I have long been of the o[...] [...]st
underappreciated and unc[...] ng
by pastors and personal st[...], [...] [...]se
we find the study of God's precepts about wisdom, knowledge, self-discipline, and the rewards thereof, boring and uninteresting. But what Jared has done in *Wisdom for Kings and Queens* is invite us to engage or, perhaps, re-engage Proverbs not as stale pedagogy but as dynamic jewels of truth that God has lovingly and graciously endowed His people with for their benefit and enjoyment in Him. In *Wisdom for Kings and Queens*, Jared has succeeded in giving Proverbs the depth of theological treatment it deserves, while presenting it in such a way that a child can understand and apply it.

— Darrell B. Harrison
Co-host of the *Just Thinking* podcast,
Dean of Social Media at Grace to You Ministries, Valencia, CA

This present age has been infected and dominated by worldly wisdom which encourages an appetite for rebellion against God and his Law. This has been the case since the fall of Adam and Eve in the garden. The Proverbs expose the faulty claim that the Bible is not relevant for this modern era of human history. In fact, in the Proverbs we see just how relevant God's Word is for us and that holy Scripture transcends time and culture. This short book by Jared Longshore is a readable volume for the family that will encourage and equip you to navigate with God's light through the darkness of our age.

— Josh Buice
Pastor of Pray's Mill Baptist Church,
Founder of G3 Conference, Douglasville, GA

The world is in want of wisdom. But where do we find it? Pastor Jared Longshore has wisely distilled and interpreted for our own times the greatest book of wisdom ever written. If the fear of the Lord is the beginning of wisdom, buying this little book must be somewhere on that same list.

— Larry Taunton
Author, Columnist, and Executive Director
of the Fixed Point Foundation

I love Proverbs, and I love what Jared has done with it through sermon and book. Back in my 1970's teaching days at Wheaton, I began each philosophy class by reading a chapter of Proverbs, a dose of divine wisdom before considering what the world's "love of wisdom" (aka "philosophy") had produced. I wish I'd had Jared's commentary handy. The language is engaging (urging us to be "wise serpents" rather than "aloof llamas," to stay out of "Crazy Town," and to beware since "You can get yourself into a whole lot of trouble in a jiffy"); the illustrative references apt (as to the work of Frank Sinatra, John Bunyan, Kate Millett, and Jordan Peterson, plus the story of Pinocchio and "coexist" bumper stickers); and the exegesis instructive (showing that Proverbs 2:5 teaches that "the fear of the LORD must be cultivated," for it "requires great effort.")

— Mark Coppenger
Author, Retired Professor of Christian Philosophy and Ethics
at the Southern Baptist Theological Seminary, Louisville, KY

This discussion of Proverbs is intense, accessible, relevant, and evangelical. Longshore's clarity of presentation and isolation of teachings shows how intensely soul-assaulting the book is on anything that tends toward the destruction of the image of God in man. No one has to wonder what either the author of Proverbs, or the author of this book about Proverbs, is aiming at. The style is clear, the illustrations are pithy and in your face. It is relevant for eternity and for our short span of time here. Eternal wisdom has invaded this world so that we will not destroy our souls through things that themselves will perish and points us to the immutable standards from the throne of God Himself. Not only is eternal wisdom unchanging, but the ways in which fallen persons pervert God's righteous law are unchanging. Such revealed descriptions about human folly and sin cannot fail to resound with a transparent note of contemporaneity. It points to the final answer in granting the eternal advantages of wisdom in Christ, who is the voice and the incarnation of wisdom. The chapters are short but pithy and even entertaining. It will make for good family discussion, one evening per chapter and will prompt the healthiest kind of conversation for wives and husbands, parents and children, and do good to the soul.

— Tom Nettles
Author, Church Historian,
Retired Professor of Church History and Historical Theology
at the Southern Baptist Theological Seminary, Louisville, KY

The wisdom in Proverbs runs deep. In this work, Jared Longshore plumbs the depths of the Proverbs to deliver a concise, robust, and thoughtful understanding of ancient wisdom so needed for today. Like the Proverbs, you'll find yourself going back to this enlightening work time and time again.

— Virgil Walker
Discipleship Pastor of Westside Church
and Co-host of the *Just Thinking* podcast, Omaha, NE

Wisdom is not for the fainthearted. For true wisdom demands truth as its center, grace as its attitude, and love as its fuel. Proverbs is replete with countless jewels of instruction for those who desire wisdom to live a life well pleasing before the Lord. As Proverbs stands in the canon of eternity, this work by Jared Longshore will help you weather the temptation to succumb to cultural relevancy and cry forth, "The fear of the Lord is the beginning of knowledge" (Proverbs 1:7). Visit and revisit this excellent work to remind yourself, your spouse, and your family that godly wisdom flows from a life anchored in Christ.

— Dustin Benge
Provost, Union School of Theology, Bridgend, Wales

Jared Longshore is wise beyond his years, which makes him the perfect pastor to produce this work on Proverbs. It's short but meaty, entertaining but weighty, and well worth your time and prayerful pondering.

— Rod D. Martin
Futurist, Tech Entrepreneur, CEO of the Martin Organization, and Member of SBC Executive Committee

About half-a-dozen times each day I find myself thinking, "I know there's a Proverb for this—I just wish I knew what it was!" God really does know how life works best. In Proverbs, he has graciously told us how to safely navigate all kinds of the real-life scenarios we encounter every day in this good but fallen world. Jared Longshore is a pastor who is passionate about helping God's people walk in that life-giving wisdom of God, and this book will help you do just that. Like the book of Proverbs, Jared shoots straight about how to make your way wisely through God's world, in writing that is clear, memorable, practical, and loaded with biblical truth. Let Jared guide you through Proverbs, and let the Wisdom of God guide you through life.

— Eric Smith
Pastor of Sharon Baptist Church, Savannah, TN

I had the privilege of hearing Dr. Longshore preach a series of messages from Proverbs on which this book is based. Those were heart-warming, joy-provoking, and Christ-honoring sermons. This book sets forth that ancient wisdom to the same effect.

— Tom Ascol
Senior Pastor of Grace Baptist Church and President of Founders Ministries, Cape Coral, FL

In 1811, John Quincy Adams commended daily Bible reading to his son, for "it is of all the books in the world that which contributes most to make men good, wise, and happy." It was not so long ago that our civil rulers, at least to some extent, feared God and sought out wisdom from his word. Today, our rulers scoff at those who take Scripture seriously and seek to expunge all vestiges of the Good Book's influence on the formation of our nation's history. It would be an understatement to say that public policy is no longer guided by true wisdom. Our rulers are ignorant of the book of revelation and blind to the book of nature. No one seeks God. Even many Christians roam aimlessly through the present moral chaos that is enveloping the land, as if they have inherited no sure foundation upon which they can build. If the foundations are destroyed, what can the righteous do?

A renewed hunger for true wisdom is the only antidote to the present chaos, and what Jared Longshore offers here is brick and mortar for laying that foundation again. As any preacher knows, wisdom literature is not the simplest to exposit but Longshore makes it look easy. In highly readable prose and a practical, devotional style, Longshore guides the reader through fifteen lessons from God's wisdom in Proverbs. These lessons not only deliver wisdom to the reader but instill in them a love for it. Its organization and lucid brevity are well-suited for the Christian's daily devotions in the morning or evening. It will strengthen you for the day ahead or act as a salve for the day behind. As Longshore says, the Lord is not stingy with the knowledge that comes only from him. He delights in disseminating wisdom, if we but seek it, and his word never returns void.

King, queen, citizen; pastor, congregant; husband, wife, son, daughter, do you find yourself adrift, in need of a map to guide you through rough seas back to shore? Then let Longshore lead you through God's wisdom for God's world. In the end, this is to be led to the generous fountain of wisdom, the water of life, Christ Jesus himself. Here is true knowledge and the peace that surpasses all understanding.

— Timon Cline
Writer at Modern Reformation and Conciliar Post,
and contributor to *By What Standard?*

WISDOM FOR
KINGS & QUEENS

WISDOM FOR
KINGS & QUEENS

JARED LONGSHORE

Published by Founders Press
P.O. Box 150931 • Cape Coral, FL • 33915
Phone: (888) 525-1689
Electronic Mail: officeadmin@founders.org
Website: http://www.founders.org

Cover design by Jaye Whitehead | Jaye Bird LLC

ISBN: 978-1-943539-22-2

For my excellent wife, Heather,
and our offspring of princes and princesses:

Livia, Hudson, Scarlett, Fuller,
Winslow, Ryle, and Eleanor.

May you rule well in the fear of God.

Contents

INTRODUCTION

"Be doers of the word, and not hearers only" (James 1:22). The apostle James said that, and he was right. God did not give us truth so we could leave it on the shelf. He gave it to us that we might live.

God told our race from the beginning to "be fruitful and multiply and fill the earth and subdue it, and have dominion" (Genesis 1:28). The apostle Peter calls Christians a "royal priesthood" tasked with proclaiming the excellencies of Him who called us out of darkness into His marvelous light (1 Peter 2:9). So when Christians live the truth, they cannot help but fill the earth with the knowledge of the Lord. They proclaim the glories of God as they live wisely.

Much of the book of Proverbs contains Solomon's counsel. He was a king, speaking often to his sons: "Hear, my son, your father's instruction, and forsake not your mother's teaching" (Proverbs 1:8). So the book is full of royal training. Kings and queens who would rule well should look regularly to this book, and that is precisely what followers of Jesus Christ are.

If we would live well, then we must live in the fear of God. We cannot even get started with a life well lived without reverence for our Creator, for "the fear of God is the beginning of wisdom" (Proverbs 9:10). Genuine fear of God cannot be accessed apart from Jesus Christ.

He is the King of Kings. He is wisdom. In Him are found all the treasures of wisdom and knowledge (Colossians 2:3). My hope is that He is exalted and you are edified by this book.

This book is devotional in nature. Use it as an aid to personal meditation on God's Word, family worship, Christian discipleship, and even evangelism and apologetics. May it help you as you look to God's wisdom for kings and queens.

1

THE BEGINNING OF THE GOOD LIFE

We cannot know anything as we ought to know it if we don't know God. We cannot deal wisely in this world without remembering this world's Creator. We cannot avoid sin as we ought to if we have no reverence for God. We cannot listen to truth the way we should without respecting the true God. Without the fear of the Lord, marriages crumble or limp along, education leads to swollen conceit, money leads to evil, work leads to frustration, loss results in depression, gain results in pride, and the list goes on. God really is the glue that holds the good life together.

THE BEGINNING OF KNOWLEDGE

To make a start in the good life, we must come to see that a body of knowledge is out there for us to know. Solomon states the reason for his book of wisdom up front—"To know wisdom and instruction, to understand words of insight" (Proverbs 1:2). Knowledge is a thing, the kind of thing that some people get and others don't. Many people have been tripped up by their disbelief in objective truth. "To each their own," they say. "I just need to be true to myself," they say. But then they stick a screwdriver in a light socket. Truth bites back. Worldly philosophers and teachers have deconstructed and dismissed objective truth. In so doing, they have produced aimless people wandering about unsure of what to do or where to go. But there is a creator who has made all that has been made. He unites all things. He is *the truth*. We are to know Him and know all revealed things (be they seen or unseen) in relation to Him. All things include lily pads, hummingbirds, sexuality, death, the human soul, angels, cheeseburgers, algebra, indoor plumbing, and anything in between.

Not only is there a body of knowledge but there is knowledge concerning wise living. God is not merely interested in filling our heads with facts. He wants us to walk in knowledge. He desires that we live well (Proverbs 1:3). God is the one who made both the world and you, and like a good chef, He knows how these two things mix to taste delightful. He knows the bad combinations too. His instruction is not only the right way, it is the best way. When people run after other gods, they end up sad. When we disregard God's teaching for our own ideas, we're left with a sour taste in our mouths. Psalm 19 says the law of the Lord revives the soul, rejoices the heart, and enlightens the eyes.

This body of knowledge we are to live by concerns our relationship to God, man, and self. Scripture speaks of righteousness, justice, and equity. Righteousness concerns what is fitting in our relationship with God. God is righteous. To have a saving relationship with Him, you must be righteous. People are terribly confused about this requirement of righteousness to know God savingly. No man can achieve this necessary righteousness. God has provided this righteousness in His Son, Jesus Christ. Those who trust Christ receive His righteousness. They receive instruction in righteousness. The Scriptures can make you wise for salvation by helping you understand this required and provided righteousness. Justice involves bringing about what is right to our fellow man. Isaiah 42:1 says Jesus will "bring forth justice to the nations." We should get knowledge so we can do right by others and care for the poor and oppressed. Equity involves having a straightforward, honorable demeanor. With this knowledge, we can learn to be the same person of character no matter what day of the week it is or who surrounds us.

Knowledge is for the simple and the wise. No one is above it. "To give prudence to *the simple*, knowledge and discretion to the youth—Let *the wise* hear and increase in learning and the one who understands obtain guidance" (Proverbs 1:4). If you're looking for a fool, find a man who thinks he is above learning, the one who says, "I've studied enough, contemplated enough, heard enough sermons, and read enough Scripture." That's a fool talking. When simple youth listen to sound words, they learn to take caution and think well. When the wise listen to sound words, they learn even more.

But here is the starting block. Here's the first step up the breathtaking mountain of knowledge—the fear of the Lord. "The fear of the LORD is the beginning of knowledge" (Proverbs 1:7). If you don't have the fear of the Lord, then you don't have a chance at getting this most precious knowledge. You can learn a lot of things, but you won't have understanding.

So, what is this fear of the Lord? Well, it is not the fear that a criminal has for the police. It is the reverence a faithful son has for a loving and righteous father. This son does not fear that his father will beat him in a drunken rage, but he does know that disobedience to his father will result in consequences, and more importantly, this son does not want to grieve his father. The fear of the Lord concerns a loving and humble reverence by which a Christian trusts his Father's word and carefully obeys His law.

The opposite of this wise God-fearer is the fool who "[despises] wisdom and instruction" (Proverbs 1:7). The fool hates learning. The fool thinks his own way is best. He ignores God. He only thinks about himself. He focuses on his desires and not God's.

If the fear of the Lord is the beginning of knowledge, then we desperately need the fear of the Lord. But since the fear of the Lord is a loving reverence for God as our *Father* that moves us to obey Him humbly, we can never experience such fear outside of Christ. Without Christ, you may fear God like a criminal does the authorities, but you can never see Him as a loving and righteous father. This holy God requires righteousness and has provided that perfection in His Son, Jesus. Jesus lived, died, and rose again. God says to trust in Him and repent of your sins. Those who do receive all the righteousness required to know God savingly.

Do you have this saving knowledge? Are you reverencing your Father? Is He in your thoughts? Do you reverence Him in your repentance? Do you reverence Him in your studies and in your work? Do you reverence Him in your recreation, your eating and drinking, your decision-making, and your relationships? Doing so is the very foundation of the good life.

THE ENTICEMENT OF SINNERS

With the foundation of the fear of the Lord laid, we can reject the enticement of sinners. But entice they will, so we must prepare. A key to preparation is knowing the enticer's tactics.

Sinners entice with murder. "My son, if sinners entice you, do not consent. If they say, 'Come with us, let us lie in wait for blood; let us ambush the innocent without reason'" (Proverbs 1:10). Now many decorous folks will say, "Well, I'm not going to get coaxed into some murderous plot." But 1 John 3:15 says, "Everyone who hates his brother is a murderer." Decent people get enticed to murder all the time. People slander others routinely and invite you to approve of the attack. Then there is the more than three hundred thousand unborn babies who have been murdered in the last four months alone. And there is immense pressure on believers to remain silent about current issues. There is rioting in the streets of America. Sinners will entice you to stay quiet about all this wickedness. They will call you a prude, a legalist, unloving, and they will tell you not to preach at them. The problem is that our King told us to preach at them, teaching them to obey.

Sinners will also entice with lavish possessions. "We shall find all precious goods, we shall fill our houses with plunder" (Proverbs 1:13). Valuable assets are neither good nor bad, but there is a problem with stealing another guy's valuable assets. Sinners will not be satisfied with what

God has given them, and they will persistently work to get you dissatisfied too. We live in a remarkably fertile land and fruitful time. Yet, we have an endless supply of malcontents. Why is this? One reason is that sinners have a discipleship program going, one that tells you at various times and in various ways that you don't have enough. "Look at his wife," they say. "Look at her husband." "Wouldn't their house be better than yours?" "Isn't their family everything you want?" "If only you had that job with all of its perks." "Things would be different if you had that amount of vacation, those opportunities, that education." Turn a deaf ear to such enticements, or you'll end up a plundering pirate.

Sinners entice at a rapid pace; they're quick about running into evil (Proverbs 1:15). You can get yourself into a whole lot of trouble in a jiffy. The remedy to their speedy enticement is the art of the plod. Proverbs 13:11 says, "Wealth gained hastily will dwindle, but whoever gathers little by little will increase it." The second half of that proverb commends steady work. The principle of plodding is broader than just storing up money. It also applies to the Christian life in general. You don't build a healthy marriage in a day. You don't produce godly kids in a moment. You don't become a generous person in an instant. This kind of stuff requires a long obedience in the same direction. So the sobering caution is this: breaking down is quicker than building. Sin breaks down fast, quick, and in a hurry. If sin has taken a sledgehammer to your hard work, don't despair. God can restore what has been lost. Even so, let every one of us stay away from the path of sinners since they're quick to evil.

The enticement of sinners is foolish, for they're digging their own grave. They are as dumb as birds flying into a net. And they spread the net for themselves. It is one thing when somebody else gets the best of you. But it's worse when you trip yourself. We should start by learning that sinners lose. That's true enough. But we should proceed to learn that the very thing sinners are after is the instrument of death. They are hungry for the electric chair. "Such are the ways of everyone who is greedy for unjust gain; it takes away the life of its possessors" (Proverbs 1:19).

The antidote to sinner's enticement is father and mother's teaching. "Hear, my son, your father's instruction, and forsake not your mother's teaching, for they are a graceful garland for your head and pendants for your neck" (Proverbs 1:8). If sons and daughters would reject the lustful call of sinners, then father and mother must teach. They must teach all that is necessary in order that their children might grow up in the nurture and admonition of the Lord. They must pray and work and go to bed tired. They must ask God for more insight and the ability to instruct their children in the way they should go. No parent knows everything there is to know. Yet God has made it the parents' responsibility to teach their children. Pray. Read. Ask others what they've done with their children. Structure your life so that you have time to teach them.

With all this enticement, what are we to do? Fear God, and "do not consent" (Proverbs 1:10). Reject the tempting words of fools. We are not to be outwitted by Satan. We are not to be ignorant of his designs. And surely, we are not to let our children grow up in the blind about the temptations they will face. Sinners will entice them and us. So mark the fruitlessness of those temptations. Don't fear them; fear God.

The Cry of Wisdom

Gratefully, the call of sinners is not the only call. There is also the call of wisdom.

Wisdom cries aloud. She is a faithful friend. She does not want people to go in bad directions. Here is encouragement to get wisdom. The deck is not stacked against you. Wisdom is not running away from you. She's for you. God has made this world, and He speaks to you through it: "The heavens declare the glory of God, and the sky above proclaims his handiwork" (Psalm 19:1). Jesus has sent out His disciples to proclaim the gospel from the housetops. They have done so. The good news has been spreading for two thousand years now. It is still on the offensive.

But wisdom is crying aloud in noisy streets and busy markets (Proverbs 1:20–21). The picture teaches us that there are many voices coming at us. If we would hear wisdom, we must tune out some of the noise at the city gates. If you don't pay attention to wisdom, then you will get swept along this noisy street. If you just go with the flow, if you gather a group of friends that are anything but spiritually minded, you will not hear wisdom. If you take daily doses of worldly counsel or mindlessly ingest movies, media, and textbooks, you will not hear wisdom.

If you will give your ear to wisdom, she promises to pour out knowledge to you. "How long, O simple ones, will you love being simple? How long will scoffers delight in their scoffing and fools hate knowledge? If you turn at my reproof, behold, I will pour out my spirit to you; I will make my words known to you" (Proverbs 1:22–23). Wisdom is the kind of generous lady who keeps on giving. And she gives more to those who turn to her. She's like Christ, who takes away from the one who is unfaithful and gives more to the faithful one. Our egalitarian ears have trouble processing this kind of thing. We think everyone on this noisy street should get the same amount of time from lady wisdom. But God knows better than we do. Wisdom pours out her spirit *to those who turn*. That's motivation to turn—and quickly.

On the flip side, if you neglect her, wisdom will laugh when your trouble comes. She reminds us of a woman who is offended in all the right ways. "Because I have called and you refused to listen, have stretched out my hand and no one has heeded, because you have ignored all my counsel and would have none of my reproof, I also will laugh at your calamity; I will mock when terror strikes you" (Proverbs 1:24–26). Don't get on wisdom's bad side. Notice the sin at this point is indifference. She charges that we refused to listen. We did not heed. We ignored. She has put her finger on our problem. We don't want to pay attention. We just don't care. We are far more interested in other things. The problem with indifference is that the world's troubles are not indifferent. Bad stuff will happen to you in this world if you do nothing. Weeds grow in the garden. Homes get dirty. Relationships fall apart. Everything needs maintenance. Without wisdom, calamity will come upon you like a whirlwind. It is "the complacency of fools [that] destroys them" (Proverbs 1:32).

If you call out for wisdom whenever you get around to it, she will not only laugh at you but she will not listen to you: "Then they will call upon me, but I will not answer; they will seek me diligently but will not find me"

(Proverbs 1:28). In other words, she says, "Don't come around knockin' on my door *now*. It's too late, buster." If you've heard this once, you've heard it a thousand times—"I just want to sin now and get Jesus later." The problem with that setup is such an attitude signals that Jesus will not answer the door for you later. Jesus will not be the quarter for you to put in the salvation slot-machine whenever you want. He is *Lord*. He calls you to embrace His wisdom humbly now. Come to Him *now*. If you harden your heart now, you have no promise that He will listen to you when you call.

If we refuse wisdom, she will not only laugh at our trouble and turn a deaf ear to us but she will let us fill up on the sour fruit of our way: "Because they hated knowledge and did not choose the fear of the LORD, would have none of my counsel and despised all my reproof, therefore they shall eat the fruit of their way, and have their fill of their own devices" (Proverbs 1:29–30). She has no problem letting us suffer the full measure of our consequences.

Wisdom is a straight talker. But it does not follow that she's a harsh lady. She's a gracious lady. Being a generous lady, she leaves us with a hopeful word: "But whoever listens to me will dwell secure and will be at ease, without dread of disaster" (Proverbs 1:33). Wisdom makes us a promise. Listen, and live. Listen, and be at ease.

Two voices are crying out for our attention. One is the enticing voice of sinners. They invite us to unjust gain, leading to death. The other is the voice of wisdom. She calls us to learn from her now so we can live. But the only way to reject the first and lend our ear to the second is by walking in the fear of the Lord.

2

WISDOM WILL DELIVER YOU

N o one wants to be a sitting duck. No one wishes to be a soft target. The bad guys look for that kind of thing. They keep an eye out for old grandmother going into the store after dark. The bad guys would be quite surprised when some of our grannies greeted them with a right hook. Granny has lived long enough to know there is trouble in the world.

Like Granny, we need to wise up. Jesus tells us to be sheep who are as "wise as serpents." We must be prepared for a fight because Jesus has sent us out "in the midst of wolves" (Matthew 10:16). Jesus has not called us to be declawed house cats. They don't do so well among wolves. Jesus has not called us to be aloof llamas chowing down unconcernedly in the open field. He has told us to be as wise as serpents. Becoming this takes work. But if you do, you'll do well amid wolves.

The point of this chapter is you need to get wisdom from the Lord for it will deliver you. Let me emphasize *from the Lord*. It comes from Him. And let me emphasize the *get*, too. You have to work, strive, and fight to get wisdom. Be slack in this, and you won't get wisdom. Be slack in this, and you won't be delivered. Be diligent in this, and you will be guarded. You will be protected from the way of the wicked that will soon be cut off.

GET WISDOM FROM THE LORD

If you pursue wisdom from the Lord, you will get it. Christians ought to receive God's instruction as children from a loving father. He tells us to get to work. There is, of course, a lie running amok today that fathers shouldn't tell their children to get to work. But that's silliness. "Work hard" is exactly what loving fathers tell their children. So, in Christ, we receive these exhortations as what we are—God's children.

First, the father says you must receive commandments: "My son, if you receive my words and treasure up my commandments with you" (Proverbs 2:1). The requirement is not to "follow your heart." The requirement is not to "look within yourself." The instruction is to receive from another. Look outside yourself to the wise Father. What are you to receive from Him? Commandments. Not advice. Not suggestions or recommendations. We are to welcome being told what to do. If we would pursue wisdom, we must be "Sir, yes, sir" kind of people. David said, "Oh, how I love your law." He said he had more understanding than his teachers because he meditated on God's law (Psalm 119:97, 99).

Second, if you would pursue wisdom, then you must think on wisdom. The wise father tells his son to make his "ear attentive to wisdom" and incline his "heart to understanding" (Proverbs 2:2). We're not going to get there by simply complying with commandments. Yes, we must obey His commandments, but we must also focus on sound words. We have to put our hearts into it. We must meditate. We must think over the truth. Applying your heart to the truth requires a disciplined and systematic approach. This kind of thing involves repetition, conversation, and thoughtfulness.

Furthermore, pursuing wisdom includes crying out for wisdom: "Yes, if you call out for insight and raise your voice for understanding" (Proverbs 2:3). If you begin thinking on Scripture, you will find a greater need for understanding. You will discover just how much you don't know about our great and mysterious God. You will see new challenges that require help from God. What are you to do? Pray. Call out for help. Lift up your voice and ask for wise people to teach you. This pursuit of wisdom includes seeking it out. You really need to get after this stuff like silver and hidden treasure. You've got to spend your energy on the search for wisdom.

How are you doing at pursuing wisdom? Be honest with yourself. How have you welcomed His commandments over the last week? Can you write a couple of paragraphs that spell out your systematic approach to meditating on God's truth? When do you do it? How do you do it? If the rhythm of your life does not include steady thinking on God's Word, what needs to change?

Our motivation to get going in the pursuit of wisdom is this: the Lord gives wisdom. "For the LORD gives wisdom; from his mouth come knowledge and understanding" (Proverbs 2:6). He is not stingy. He delights to supply us with knowledge. James 1:5 says, "If any of you lacks wisdom, let him ask God, who gives generously to all without reproach, and it will be given him." But make sure you get wisdom *from the Lord*. There is an earthly wisdom, but that wisdom is no good. If you're going after knowledge so you can boast, then you are going after the earthly kind, which is not only unspiritual but demonic.

God gives wisdom to a certain kind of person. He gives to the upright and those who walk in integrity. If you love God and follow His commands, He will help you do so more and more. "He stores up sound wisdom" for such people (Proverbs 2:7). He resources those who do His will. God-doubters, on the other hand, are double-minded and unstable. James says such people should not expect to receive anything from God (James 1:7–8).

God not only gives wisdom to the righteous but in so doing, He preserves them. God guards the paths of justice and watches over the way of His saints (Proverbs 2:7). The saints do get into some sticky situations sometimes. You will have your share of trials. We have no promise that He will preserve us from the steep road. But He will watch over us along that road.

In the Old Testament, the nation of Judah was being attacked by surrounding nations. Judah's king, Jehoshaphat, looked to God in prayer, saying, "O our God, will you not execute judgment on them? For we are powerless against this great horde that is coming against us. *We do not know what to do, but our eyes are on you*" (2 Chronicles 20:12). Your battles belong to God. Jehoshaphat illustrates the posture we should have when pursuing wisdom. If we don't get wisdom from God, we're simply not going to get it.

If we pursue wisdom, then we will know the fear of the Lord. We have this as a promise from God. If you seek knowledge, "then you will understand the fear of the LORD" (Proverbs 2:5). Do you want the fear of the Lord? God promises that you can attain it by pursuing wisdom. The fear of the Lord must be cultivated. God gives this good and right fear. At the same time, we must pursue it diligently if we're going to possess it. And it *is* worth possessing. "Wisdom will come into your heart, and [this] knowledge will be pleasant to your soul" (Proverbs 2:10).

WISDOM WILL DELIVER YOU

The knowledge of God is a precious treasure in and of itself. But it is also essential to see that this knowledge will deliver you. It delivers us *from* something and *to* something. Wisdom rescues us *from* the evil man and woman; it delivers us *unto* the way of good men and women.

First, the father says wisdom will deliver you from the evil man. The evil man speaks perverted things (Proverbs 2:12). He not only speaks lies, he speaks perversion. Proverbs 10:32 says, "The lips of the righteous know what is acceptable, but the mouth of the wicked, what is perverse." So perverse speech is the opposite of acceptable speech. The evil man speaks unacceptable things. His speech is not merely unacceptable to the Christian's ears. The point is not only that some godly old saint will object, saying, "I'm not going to tolerate this kind of talk." That's good and right but not the main idea. It is instead that the evil man's speech is unacceptable *to God*. The wicked man stores up wrath with every perverted word. And here's the kicker: all the evil man's words are perverted. He cannot get anything right. Romans 3:13 says the venom of vipers is under his tongue.

Ladies, evil men have told you that your most important beauty is external. Evil men have said to you that growing old is nothing but a drag. Evil men have told you that working quietly with your hands in your home is unfulfilling and unimportant. Evil men will corruptly affirm you when you are in a dangerous way rather than speak honest words of loving correction. Evil husbands twist Scripture to rule harshly over their wives. That's what weak-willed, abdicating, perverted men do. But if you get the fear of the Lord, the wisdom that comes from Him, you will be delivered from the sick speech of evil men.

We should also be aware of the evil man's crooked walk. He "forsake[s] the path of uprightness to walk in the ways of darkness" (Proverbs 2:13). The evil man not only speaks perversion but walks in it. He has a certain strut marked by darkness. The evil man has developed wicked patterns, customs, and traditions. He doesn't even realize how backward his ways are.

Men, like Isaiah we dwell amid unclean people. Too often the unclean man sets the pace with his crooked steps and we follow. The main problem with his walk is his general direction, which is toward godlessness. He's got all sorts of evils that spring up in the way he usually heads. He spends his money as well as his time in God-disregarding ways. He relates to his family in God-disregarding ways. He both does his work and recreates in God-disregarding ways. We have adopted some of his customs unthinkingly because we cannot imagine doing things a different way. But if we get the fear of the Lord, we will be delivered from the evil man's crooked walk.

There is another thing about the evil man to look out for. He delights in perversity. He "rejoice[s] in doing evil and delight[s] in the perverseness of evil" (Proverbs 2:14). The ugliness resides in his heart. He likes what is twisted and deformed. God has given him up to a debased mind, to foolish passions. He is like a dog returning to its vomit. Scripture says the heart is deceitfully wicked above all things; it is so bad that no one can understand it (Jeremiah 17:9). The evil man cannot help but dangle sinful pleasures before others. He satisfies his lusts and welcomes others to do the same. We must prepare then. The evil man will woo us to perversion. But if you get the fear of the Lord, if you cultivate the knowledge of God, you will be delivered from the evil man's corruption.

Wisdom will not only deliver us from the evil man but the evil woman as well. We will need protection against her. "So you will be delivered from the forbidden woman, from the adulteress" (Proverbs 2:16). Some translations call her "strange," which gets at the meaning more completely. This evil woman is foreign to all that is right, good, beautiful, and true. She's a stranger to God's law and ought to be a stranger to us. She's perverted like the evil man. She is a distorted and disfigured woman. She ought to make the godly lose their appetite.

She flatters with smooth words. The problem is not only her words but her aggressive pursuit of you. She promises to satisfy you. She speaks to you with her tight and revealing clothes. She speaks to you through the television and the internet. The wise father knows we will fall to her seduction if we are not ready to stand against her advances. There are strange women everywhere in our society. You will not be able to go a day without her annoying you. Get the fear of the Lord, and flee. Men have no right to pull an Adam and blame their wives if they fall to the smooth words of the strange woman. It was clearly wrong when our first father did that, and it is still wrong today.

That is true, and this is also: wives are their husband's helpers. It's the wife's love that her husband should be intoxicated with (Proverbs 5:19). He ought to know where home is. She should be to him the opposite of the strange woman; that is the familiar one.

We live in a day of utter sexual chaos. This evil man and woman have perverted things so terribly that it is now much harder for single women to get married. Men are disincentivized to marry. Our society has "frameth mischief by a law" (Psalm 94:20 KJV). A man's wife can do away with his children against his will. His wife can divorce him even if he has done no wrong. The woman's role as a helper to her husband has been so eviscerated many men are trained to think a wife is a burden rather than an aid. Scores of single men are sexually immoral outside of wedlock, so they see no reason to be in it. None of this is right. Yet it is the lay of the land.

It is a situation in which many single women may be greatly tempted to bitterness, to throw up their hands and become the strange woman themselves. Pursue the fear of the Lord, and you will be delivered.

Single men need to join the resistance to these wicked schemes. Get a full-time job. Keep it. Get a house. Get a wife. Then seek to have children. Don't be emasculated into laziness and indirection by this sexually promiscuous climate.

The evil woman is not only a flatterer. She is a covenant breaker. She "forsakes the companion of her youth and forgets the covenant of her God" (Proverbs 2:17). She's an unfaithful woman. Unfaithfulness is not pretty. It's not cute. This strange woman is untethered from relationship with God. There couldn't be anything more ugly.

As a result of her covenant-disloyalty, her home goes down to death. "For her house sinks down to death, and her paths to the departed" (Proverbs 2:18). Go to the strange woman if you want to die. This woman's home is a hellhole. She will take your mind down to death. She will take your affections down to death. She will take your manhood down to death. She will take you, body and soul, down to death. There will not be any of you left if you walk in her paths.

That's because she does not let her victims out of her death trap. "None who go to her come back, nor do they regain the paths of life" (Proverbs 2:19). We are prone to think, "I will be the one to escape. I will visit just once at nightfall and make it back to the path of life." No, you won't.

The knowledge of God will not only deliver us from evil but will also keep us in the way of good men and women. "So you will walk in the way of the good and keep to the paths of the righteous" (Proverbs 2:20). The one who fears the Lord loves the fellowship of God-fearers. David says in Psalm 16:3, "As for the saints in the land, they are the excellent ones, in whom is all my delight."

The fear of the Lord produces love for the church. What good news! We don't have to walk through the wolf pack alone. If your love for God's people is at a low ebb, then cultivate the fear of the Lord.

Get the fear of the Lord for it will deliver you. There is a lot at stake here. "For the upright will inhabit the land, and those with integrity will remain in it, but the wicked will be cut off from the land, and the treacherous will be rooted out of it" (Proverbs 2:21–22). Life and death are set before us. If we would remain in the land, then we must walk in holiness. If we join the covenant-breaking wicked, we will be cut off unto eternal death. Do you want to remain in the land? Then pursue wisdom from the Lord. He gives it to those who call out in faith—every time. He is faithful. He will do it.

You may say, "I have no right to it. I don't deserve the fear of the Lord. I've joined in the perversion of the evil man and evil woman." Ah! You are correct. You have no right to it yourself. But you have every right to it in Christ! Jesus has never walked in the path of sinners or sat in the seat of scoffers. He has never joined in the perverted speech of the evil man or visited the strange woman's home. In Him are found all the treasures of wisdom and knowledge. Jesus, the Son of God, lived, died, and rose again. So trust Him in the fear of the Lord. Seek Him. You'll get the fear of the Lord and live forever in the good land.

3

God's Wisely Designed World

If you keep an eye out, you will notice this in the world: man wants to go his own way. We want to march to the beat of our own drum. It was not for nothing that Frank Sinatra sang his song about man doing life his own way.

Such a way of life may sound good at first. We can appreciate taking blows for a righteous cause. But if we're honest, when we've done things our way, we haven't exactly suffered for righteousness' sake but stupidity's. If our way is not God's way, then it is not only wrong, it's dangerous. If your way is to drive through red lights, then you're going to take a whole lot more than a blow. If your way is to jump off tall buildings with a bed sheet, thinking you can fly, then you're going to experience a lot more than bumps and bruises. Pride is a poison that leads man to ruin.

This is God's world, so His ways work best. God made this world in a certain way. You can try to kick against the way He made it. But that won't work out well for you. On the other hand, if you learn from Him, if you trust and obey Him, then you will be blessed.

Imagine you got a brand-new jet boat, and the chief designer of this boat joined you for your first ride. How foolish would it be to say, "I understand you made this boat to work a certain way, but I want to try putting water in the gas tank"? Or "I heard that you set this boat up so that if I turn the wheel to the right, it goes right. But, you know, I like to do things my way. I need to go right, but I'm going to pull this wheel to the left." We live this way far too often. But things would go quite a lot better on the boat if we followed the wisdom of the designer.

In this chapter, I want to unpack this truth with seven smaller ones.

THE WISE FIND GOD'S FAVOR

First, the wise find God's favor (Proverbs 3:4). Not everyone finds success in the eyes of God, but the wise do. Stop and consider that for a moment. Many claim that everyone receives God's favor. But His Word says you have to be something to get it. You have to be wise.

To be wise, we must not forget the Father's commands. Growing wise requires storing up God's law in our hearts. It is far too easy to forget what our Lord has said. But there is good reason to remember His instruction. We should remember God's commands because they are life-giving (Proverbs 3:2). They bring length of days and years of life—peaceful ones to boot. If we take Him at His Word here, then surely, we will keep His commandments. Adam and Eve went wrong at just this point in the garden. They did not believe God when He said the forbidden fruit was no good for them.

But we don't merely keep God's commands in a wooden way. We obey from the heart, and we obey in faith. We must keep steadfast love: "Let not steadfast love and faithfulness forsake you" (Proverbs 3:3). Our submission to God's law springs from a heart that loves Him resolutely. Heartless obedience won't do.

And what is the reward for lovingly heeding God's commands? Divine favor. What a life! It's a life of good success. Moreover, our favor is not only with God but also with man. The vertical and horizontal favor should not take us by surprise. Men, in general, are pleased with neighbors who don't murder them. They like folks who don't sneak into their homes at night and steal their stuff. Come to find out, God's ways are good for human relationships. Of course, this favor with man doesn't mean that every person will like you. Many will hate you because they hate God and themselves. Even so, in the main, the wise flourish in the sight of God and man.

The Wise Live toward God

Second, the wise live toward God. If we would be wise, then we must depend on God, not ourselves. We should trust in the Lord with all our hearts. We rely on Him and not our own ideas. Undoubtedly, one of the quickest tests to see if we are doing this is to examine our prayers. Prayer demonstrates that we are looking to God for help. Those who pray put their confidence in God. Those who do not pray put their confidence somewhere else.

We must acknowledge God in all we do. The Christian possesses a continual awareness of God. The wise understand that God is always with them. He is watching. He is listening. He matters in every situation, be it work or recreation, family or friends, easy or hard. He can direct our path through any dark valley because He is with us in that darkness with rod and staff to comfort us.

So the wise are not wise in their own eyes. They rather revere the one true Master and Creator. Many people claim that such fear is wrong. They say that the fear of God is contrary to His love. They argue that fearing God is a dark and miserable way to live. But the fear of the Lord brings "healing to [our] flesh and refreshment to [our] bones" (Proverbs 3:8).

Along with fearing the Lord, we must honor the Lord with our wealth (Proverbs 3:9). When we give to God, we recognize Him as the one who has given us everything. We offer Him the firstfruits because He's the one who makes the fruit grow in the first place. In the New Testament, we hear the question, "What do you have that you did not receive?" (1 Corinthians 4:7). The wise know the answer is *nothing*. We have received everything. So we give back to the One who has given to us. When you do so, "then your barns will be filled with plenty, and your vats will be bursting with wine" (Proverbs 3:10).

As we live Godward, we must not despise the Father's discipline. We should not be weary of His correction, because the Lord disciplines the one He loves. The wisdom of this world says, "I don't want God's rod of correction. I don't want to be trapped. I want to be free to do whatever I want." The wise, however, welcome God's discipline while remembering His great love for them.

THE WISE GET GOD'S BLESSING

Third, the wise get God's blessing. Wisdom provides blessing *if you get it* (Proverbs 3:13). Mark that. One kind of person is blessed: the one who finds wisdom.

Wisdom not only provides a blessing, it provides a big blessing. The gain from wisdom is better than silver and gold (Proverbs 3:14). One reason people don't gain as much as they could is because they don't know where the biggest gains are. We all play with limited resources. There is only so much time and money for each of us. So, you must decide. Will you spend resources on getting wisdom or some other endeavor? Will you pursue God's wisdom or take a season pursuing godlessness? People wander off into godlessness because they think it will pay out. They are going after their pleasure. But such people have forgotten the important thing. Riches are found in wisdom.

What kind of big blessing does wisdom produce? "Long life is in her right hand" (Proverbs 3:16). Honor is in her left hand. Her paths are pleasant and full of peace. "She is a tree of life" (Proverbs 3:18). We find a tree of life at the beginning of the Bible in the garden of Eden. We see a tree of life again at the very end of the Bible in the book of Revelation when Christ returns. This tree of life is *life with God*. So, the better question is "What kind of blessing does wisdom *not* produce?" The wise get the very blessing of life with God, which is to say they get every blessing.

God Designed the World in Wisdom

The fourth truth explains why God's ways work best. It explains why the wise are favored, Godward, and blessed. Put simply, God designed the world by His wisdom.

God founded the world by wisdom. Psalm 24:1 says, "The earth is the Lord's and the fullness thereof, the world and those who dwell therein." God has established this world with its operations. There are physical and spiritual realities that simply cannot be denied. They can be ignored to our detriment, but our ignorance of them will not change them. If you abandon wisdom, you run against the very structure by which the world was made.

God not only *founded* the world but *governs* the world in wisdom. Proverbs 3:20 speaks of Him breaking open the deeps and dropping down the dew. God keeps on ruling over His world by wisdom. He sends forth both the dangerous bursting forth of waters and the nurturing giving of rain.

Thus, there is a reason you need water to live, why you cannot jump up and touch the top of a skyscraper, and why no one wants to live in cities full of murderers. God's wisely designed world naturally demonstrates that when two people stay together in marriage their children are more likely to flourish. His wise design of the world is the reason why the true gospel improves a land when the people in that land believe it. God made the world such that pride goes before a fall and the humble are exalted. All these things occur because there is a God who reigns over heaven and earth. He is good, and His ways are good! Proof of His existence is all around us.

The Wise Get God's Protection

Fifth, those who live in God's wisdom get His protection. But we must hold on to wisdom: "My son, do not lose sight of these—keep sound wisdom and discretion" (Proverbs 3:21). We must not lose wisdom once we've found it. Wisdom can slip away. We can run well for a bit but be hindered down the road.

If we keep wisdom, it will protect our lives (Proverbs 3:22). Wisdom will be life to us. If Adam and Eve had kept wisdom in the garden, their lives would have been protected from the curse of death. All of us now must face physical death, but we all don't have to face spiritual death. Wisdom can protect us from that.

Wisdom protects us from stumbling (Proverbs 3:23). There are many dangers, toils, and snares in this life. Many things can trip you up. The enemy is an expert at laying snares for us. But you can follow Christ each day protected from these many traps if you get wisdom.

Wisdom will also protect you from anxiety. Proverbs 3:24 says, "If you lie down, you will not be afraid; when you lie down, your sleep will be sweet." The person who sees that God rules this world can rest well. Each person much choose between two fears: the anxiety-ridding fear of God or the anxiety-ridden fear of man.

Wisdom will protect you from fearful destruction (Proverbs 3:25). The wicked will be ruined with sudden terror. We know that it is appointed for man to die, and then comes judgment (Hebrews 9:27). God's judgment upon the wicked is one of eternal ruin. This dreadful destruction comes upon all those who do not trust Christ. But the wise are protected from this sudden terror. The wise find that it is God Himself who protects them. The Lord is the confident guardian of His people who will not let them be destroyed.

THE WISE LIVE TOWARD MAN

We saw earlier that the wise live toward God, but it is also true that they live toward man. That is the sixth truth.

The wise do what is just in their relationships (Proverbs 3:27). If a man does a job for us, we should readily pay him his due. If a woman does an honorable deed, we should respond with appropriate praise. When you hear of a worthy initiative, and it is within your power to contribute, you should contribute.

We should not wait to do good (Proverbs 3:28). We cannot say, "I've got the money to pay the light bill that is due, but I'm going to hold on to that money for a few more days. The light company can just wait." No, the wise pay what is due when it is due.

If we would be wise, then we must not plan evil against our neighbor. The wise understand that God made the world in wisdom. He created each one in His own image. God sees all and knows when a wicked idea enters the mind.

Wise people do not envy an oppressor: "Do not envy a man of violence and do not choose any of his ways" (Proverbs 3:31). People envy the violent man for his power and possessions. But the wise know better than to long for such a life. The oppressor has not only pushed down others, he has pushed down God's laws. Those laws tend to snap back with authority. The oppressor is working against the grain of the universe. He seeks to suppress the truth, which never works in the end. His power and possessions will turn to ashes in his mouth. God's ways will be justified in the end.

The wise live among men, remembering that the devious person is an abomination to the Lord (Proverbs 3:32). The devious person snakes his way around the God-established order of creation. He will not be successful in the end. God is right to abominate such people, for He is the one who established this world with its structure. The devious rebel against that very structure, the order of creation.

God Favors the Wise

With our seventh truth, we end up where we began. Our first principle was the wise find God's favor. Our last truth is that God favors the wise.

God curses the wicked but blesses the righteous. He is pre-committed to doing so. The fact that He does so accords with the very way He has founded the world. Psalm 1:6 says, "The Lord knows the way of the righteous, but the way of the wicked will perish." Whoever came up with "Nice guys finish last" simply didn't have the full picture in view.

God scorns the scorners, "but to the humble he gives favor" (Proverbs 3:34). Isaiah 66:2 says, "But this is the one to whom I will look: he who is humble and contrite in spirit and trembles at my word." In the words of the wise man, "The wise will inherit honor, but fools get disgrace" (Proverbs 3:35).

This is God's world, so His ways work best. The wise find God's favor because God favors the wise. The wise live toward God and man. The wise get God's blessing and protection.

As you go about following God's ways, remember, Christ is the truly wise man. He knows God's favor. He loved God and man perfectly. He received God's protection and blessing. In Him are found all the treasures of wisdom and knowledge. Indeed, He is God, the One who, with His Father, founded the earth in wisdom.

4

GET SERIOUS ABOUT GETTING WISDOM

We will be significantly helped in life when we realize that the devil is a liar. He has been calling sweet bitter and bitter sweet from the beginning. He got our first parents to believe his lies. No man has evaded the impact of that deception. From Dan to Beersheba, people are now muddled about what is good and what is not. Such confusion is a terrible curse. You pursue what you think is good, but on payday, you get garbage. Death is what sin pays its employees on the first and the fifteenth—"The wages of sin is death" (Romans 6:23).

The point of this chapter is to tell the truth about what is good and to encourage you to get it. Put simply, wisdom is a priceless treasure, so get serious about getting it. This exhortation could not be more fitting for us today. Let's be honest—the train has gone off the tracks. We have manifestly entered Crazy Town. We have officials shutting down a school's father-daughter dance because it excludes other genders, and college professors unsure which gender pronoun to use when addressing students. Leaders at the highest levels of public office are unwilling to protect life.

We do not know up from down or right from left. And insanity is never a good long-term strategy.

What are Christians to do in such foolish and evil days? Get wisdom fast, quickly, and in a hurry.

Wisdom Is Good and Hard to Get

It is one thing to know something is good. It is another to know it is hard to get. When these combine, the race is on. Consider the goodness of wisdom.

First, wisdom enriches. The wise father says to his son, "I give you good precepts" (Proverbs 4:2). If the father gave imprudent precepts, then the son would have reason not to listen. But the wise instruction of the father is valuable. We hear of the richness of wisdom in Proverbs 3:13–14: "Blessed is the one who finds wisdom, and the one who gets understanding, for the gain from her is better than gain from silver and her profit better than gold." No man in his right mind would turn down a bag full of silver and gold. Likewise, we ought not turn away from a bag of wisdom. If the two bags were before you, which would you choose? The text says that one who chooses the latter gains the most. The gain is not primarily monetary. The wise are enriched comprehensively—"My son, eat honey, for it is good, and the drippings of the honeycomb are sweet to your taste. Know that wisdom is such to your soul" (Proverbs 24:13–14).

Wisdom not only enriches. It also protects. "Do not forsake her [wisdom], and *she will keep you*; love her, and *she will guard you*" (Proverbs 4:6). Wisdom is like honey, but it is also like a fortress. We need sound words to shield us from worldly propaganda, the temptation of the devil, and dumb ideas that rise right out of our own flesh. If you get wisdom, you can stand against the enemy. He will fire his arrows at you, and you will deflect them with understanding. How dreadful it will be for those who laugh at the teaching of wisdom's protection when they find themselves face-to-face with the most vicious enemy they have ever seen. On that day, they will have nothing with which to defend themselves.

Third, wisdom exalts. "Prize her highly, and *she will exalt you*; she *will honor you*" (Proverbs 4:8). Wisdom always lifts up. You can bank on it. The person who gets wisdom will do what is honorable and, in the end, be recognized for it. The pursuit of fame and stardom is the distortion of this principle. Those who lust after glory that comes from man forsake the pursuit of wisdom. In the end, such people will be sitting in the worst seats at the table.

Along with exalting, wisdom beautifies. "She will place on your head *a graceful garland*; she will bestow on you *a beautiful crown*" (Proverbs 4:9). Wisdom will bring marvelous realities into your life. If you don't get wisdom, then your life will be dull, drab, and dreary. If you get wisdom, your life will be full of the opposite. You will look upon glorious, splendid, and magnificent things.

But wisdom is not only good. It is also hard to get. Getting wisdom requires several things from us. It requires paying attention. "Hear O sons, a father's instruction, *and be attentive*, that you may gain insight" (Proverbs 4:1). Paying attention is commanded by God. Admittedly, it is a command we often fail to meet. Who hasn't listened to the teacher in class while getting lost in a daydream? Acknowledging our distracted hearts and minds reminds us that it is a God-wrought miracle every time we pay attention to God's Word. Paying attention is tough but necessary, and it is all the tougher because we are being trained in mindlessness. There are educational strategies that say you shouldn't require a child to focus on a subject for more than a few minutes. You can find seminary professors who say to preach short messages with intermittent video clips. Some young people are scrolling themselves into oblivion on smartphones. And God says, "Pay attention."

Getting wisdom also requires being resolved to get it. "The beginning of wisdom is this: Get wisdom, *and whatever you get*, get insight" (Proverbs 4:7). The father speaks with great fervency here. If his sons are going to have any shot at getting wisdom, they must know up front that they need it. They must determine to lay hold of wisdom no matter the cost. When Navy SEAL recruits are lined up for training and asked, "Are you resolved to complete this training?" the response does not come back, "Well, maybe." If it does, then they hear only two words: "Go home." In the same way, getting wisdom requires determination. It is the kind of thing that requires a precommitment to getting it. No one floats their way to godly wisdom.

Jonathan Edwards was a minister of the gospel who lived three hundred years ago. He wrote seventy resolutions expressing his commitment to live for God. In the opening, he reminds himself to read them over once a week. Here are just two: "Resolved, to do whatever I think to be my duty and most for the good and advantage of mankind in general." "Resolved, to endeavor to obtain for myself as much happiness, in the other world, as I possibly can, with all the power, might, vigor, and vehemence, yea violence, I am capable of, or can bring myself to exert, in any way that can be thought of." [1] Getting wisdom requires this kind of holy ambition.

Getting wisdom is hard because doing so requires continual remembering: "Let your heart *hold fast*. . . . Do not *forget*, and do not *turn away*. . . . *Do not forsake* her" (Proverbs 4:4–6). After getting wisdom, we may loosen our grip, forget what we have heard, and neglect sound teaching. The pursuit of wisdom is an endurance race. Many people can go for *a* run, but not many can string those runs together over a lifetime. Getting wisdom is hard because you must go on getting it again and again.

If you are going to get wisdom, then you must love it. The wise father tells his son to love wisdom (Proverbs 4:6). He tells him to "prize her" and "embrace her" (Proverbs 4:8). You can't get wisdom without a heart change. You can't get wisdom without the miracle of the new birth wherein God removes your heart of stone and gives you a heart of flesh. You can't get wisdom without God inflaming your love for what is good, true, and beautiful. All attempts of attaining wisdom will fail without love for God and His ways. Where does that leave us? Desperately in need of God's grace that we might get that priceless treasure called wisdom.

Two Paths before You

Not only is wisdom good as well as hard to get, there are only two roads before us. The stakes are high. There is the way of wisdom and the way of foolishness. There is no third path, no middle road. All roads do not lead to glory. Let's first look at the way of wisdom, then we will observe the path of folly.

The first thing we see about the way of wisdom is that it is the way of uprightness. "I have taught you the way of wisdom; I have led you in the paths of uprightness" (Proverbs 4:11). The way of wisdom is the way of obeying God's good and right laws. "I will praise you with an upright heart, *when I learn your righteous rules*" (Psalm 119:7). We are living in God's world. He set up the standards here. Things go well when we obey Him. God delights in those who walk uprightly, and He takes "pleasure in uprightness" (1 Chronicles 29:17).

Now our problem is set cleanly before us. If the way of wisdom is the way of uprightness, then apart from Christ, none of us are on the way of wisdom, because none of us are upright. "For all have sinned and fall short of the glory of God" (Romans 3:23). Sin has laid every one of us low. We are anything but righteous left to ourselves. But God has made a way for us to enter the way of wisdom. He sent the Upright One, Jesus Christ. Jesus lived a sinless life. He knew God's right rules and kept them. He died for sinners to wash us clean. He has risen again. Those who trust Christ get His uprightness and set their feet on the way of wisdom.

That gospel is good news because the way of wisdom is the way of progress. "When you walk, your step will not be hampered, and if you run, you will not stumble" (Proverbs 4:12). No one likes getting tripped up when you are trying to go somewhere. Yet, that is precisely what sin does. Those on the way of wisdom are free to pursue God and the things of God. They are fruitful. They accomplish God's plans for themselves, others, and the world.

On the way of wisdom, this righteous progress gets better and better. "But the path of the righteous is like the light of dawn, which shines brighter and brighter until full day" (Proverbs 4:18). Those on the way of wisdom are moving forward into greater and greater light. The best is always yet to come for those on the righteous path. This path is the path of hope. Those on the way of wisdom can expect great things from God, and they won't be disappointed. If you are on this particular road, you simply cannot dream up anything greater than what God will actually do. He is able to do far more than all that we ask or even think. This is the road you want to be on.

The other road is the foolish way. Those who travel on it hunger and thirst for wickedness. They "eat the bread of wickedness and drink the wine of violence" (Proverbs 4:17). They not only practice wickedness and violence; evil is their meat and drink. They have an appetite for this kind of thing. Sin has ravaged mankind. We're not in a situation in which we sometimes do some things that are not so good. If only that were our problem. No, we've been decimated by sin. Mankind, apart from Christ, is depraved throughout.

What then comes of those on the foolish way? They are ignorantly going nowhere. "The way of the wicked is like deep darkness; they do not know over what they stumble" (Proverbs 4:19). It is one thing to be ignorant. It is another to be going nowhere. But it is a terrible condition when you are ignorantly going nowhere. The wicked way is a way of darkness, so the people on that path stumble. They are not making any headway and can't tell you what they are tripping over.

But mark this about these pitiful travelers. They long to make others stumble. "They cannot sleep unless they have done wrong; they are robbed of sleep unless *they have made someone stumble*" (Proverbs 4:16). Misery loves company. Christians, especially parents of children still in the home, must have their eyes wide open to this truth. "The companion of fools will suffer harm" (Proverbs 13:20). It is hard enough for adults to choose friends wisely—a thing that should be done, by the way: "The righteous should choose his friends carefully" (Proverbs 12:26 NKJV). Many in the way of folly want us as friends. They want your children as friends. And they are eager to make all of us stumble.

So, what should we do with this way of foolishness? Get away from it: "Do not enter the path of the wicked, and do not walk in the way of evil. Avoid it; do not go on it; turn away from it and pass on" (Proverbs 4:14–15). "Do not enter"—that is, don't even get started down that road.

"Do not walk in that way"—you shouldn't be on that road in the first place. But if you find yourself on it, stop walking that way. "Avoid it"—keep your distance. There is no reason to get close or to gaze curiously over at the way of the wicked. "Turn away"—don't only avoid it, show them your back. Set your face in an entirely different direction. Do not concern yourself in any regard with the worthless way of the fool. Finally, "pass on"—once you have avoided the fool and turned your back on him, put feet to pavement. Get going in the right direction. Burn rubber. Get moving. Run. Flee.

In John Bunyan's *Pilgrim's Progress*, a man named Christian lives in the City of Destruction. He discovers a burden on his back. An evangelist tells him that he can be saved from the wrath to come if he flees to the wicket gate. Christian's wife and children thought he had gone mad, so as Christian began to flee to the wicket gate, they came out and cried after him to persuade him to come back. But Christian put his fingers in his ears and ran on crying, "Life! Life! Eternal life!" He looked not behind him but fled. Would you be wise? Then say, "Good riddance!" to the fools who would stumble you.

Focus All Your Energies on Getting Wisdom

You must employ everything you are in the pursuit of wisdom. You must stand guard at every gate.

Guard your ears: "My son, be attentive to my words; *incline your ear to my sayings*" (Proverbs 4:20). God has much to say about our hearing. He is, after all, the God who speaks. It was in the beginning that God said, "Let there be light." He spoke to our first parents Adam and Eve. He sent His Son, Jesus Christ, as the Word. Jesus, while on earth, said, "He who has ears to hear, let him hear" (Matthew 11:15). When Jesus took Peter, James, and John up the Mount of Transfiguration, God spoke in a glorious cloud, saying of Christ, "This is my Chosen One, listen to him!" (Luke 9:35). If you would be wise, then you must listen to Christ's Word. What is it you incline your ear to?

Guard your eyes: "Let them not escape from your sight" (Proverbs 4:21). "Let your eyes look directly forward, and your gaze be straight before you" (Proverbs 4:25). Jesus teaches that if the eye is healthy, your whole body will be full of light. But if your eye is bad, your whole body will be full of darkness. David says in the Psalms, "I will not set before my eyes anything that is worthless" (Psalm 101:3). How many have walked the way of the fool by setting worthless things before their eyes? Instead of empty things, let us set Christ and His ways before our eyes. David said, "I have set the LORD always before me" (Psalm 16:8).

Guard your heart: "Keep your heart with all vigilance, for from it flow the springs of life" (Proverbs 4:23). This instruction does not concern the organ in our chest but the core of our intellectual and emotional being. Beware when you desire what God has forbidden. Ensure that you think straight and align your affections with the truth. The battle is hottest at the heart. Everything else flows from it. And it is the place where we see how desperately we need God, because our hearts will run after all kinds of idols without His grace.

Guard your mouth: "Put away from you crooked speech, and put devious talk far from you" (Proverbs 4:24). It has been said that it is better to remain silent and be thought a fool than to open your mouth and remove all doubt! While that's not in the Bible, it squares up pretty nicely with some of what the Bible says about our speaking. Lying is not the way to wisdom and blessing. Whether it comes from your own mouth or you spend time listening to the devious speech of others, crooked speech is the way to folly and destruction.

Guard your feet: "Ponder the path of your feet; then all your ways will be sure. Do not swerve to the right or to the left; turn your foot away from evil" (Proverbs 4:26–27). You must pay close attention to where you are going. If you want a sure way, if you want to walk on a good path, then don't go on the evil road. If you ignore your surroundings when you are on a hike in the woods, you can get lost in a hurry. Nightfall is an unwelcome guest to those who have neglected the path of their feet. How many people have found themselves in a far country because they ignored their spiritual surroundings? Are you further down the road of the Christian life today than you were last year? Are you in closer communion with God than you were two months ago? Ponder the path of your feet if you would get wisdom.

Wisdom is a priceless treasure, so we should get serious about getting it. Wisdom comes from God, and it is found in Christ. Call out to Him for it. Look to Christ. Listen to Christ. Pursue Christ. Call out to Christ. Here are the wisest words that have ever graced this earth: Christ Jesus came to save sinners. He lived, died, and rose again. Those who trust in Him will have eternal life.

Get Him, and you'll get wisdom.

5

Sexual Sin Kills

We can get ourselves into a whole heap of trouble if we listen to the wrong people. That is what happened to a little wooden boy in Carlo Collodi's classic book, *The Adventures of Pinocchio*. At one point in the story, Pinocchio has just nearly escaped being roasted on a fire. He's heading back to his home and father with five gold coins. But on his way, he meets a sneaky fox who pretends he cannot walk and a devious cat who pretends he cannot see.

They try to get their victim to turn aside, but Pinocchio really wants to be getting home. "The worse for you!" says the fox. "Yes, the worse for you," echoes the cat. "You're throwing away a golden opportunity," they say. The fox proceeds to tell the wooden boy of Dodo Land where he can grow a beautiful tree clustered with thousands of coins. All he has to do is bury his five gold coins in the Field of Miracles, water the ground where they lay, and sprinkle a pinch of salt over the spot. Pinocchio goes with this sly pair only to find himself alone one night on a dark road. Despite his self-confidence, two cloaked assassins (with tails) assault him for his money.

37

You, Christian, are like Pinocchio. You are on a journey to your Father. You will meet with sneaky thieves who desire to turn you off the path of life. One particular bill of goods the sly fox sells us is the promise of pleasure through sexual sin. The devil promises riches in the Dodo Land of sexual immorality. "Come aside," he says, "and I'll turn your five-coin pleasure into a thousand." The truth is he is going to mug you in the dark.

God loves us and does not want us to be fooled by the schemes of the devil. He gives us a sober warning, a warning that flows out of His desire that we be rich. What is that warning? Sexual sin kills. If you give yourself to sexual sin, you won't get happiness and life. You will get sorrow and death. Consider four words of counsel: Pay attention. Avoid the strange woman. Embrace your wife. Fear God.

PAY ATTENTION

Sexual sin kills, so pay attention. Particularly, pay attention to wisdom. "My son, be attentive to my wisdom; incline your ear to my understanding" (Proverbs 5:1). We live in a distracted age. The enemy works hard to keep people going from one thing to the next. He does not want us to stop and consider the path we are on. He does not want us to look up to the heavens and ponder why we are here. If you're going to pay attention to wisdom, then you're going to be out of step with much of modern culture. You've been born into a society that couldn't find wisdom if it smacked them in the face. They lack the tools required to get it. They lack the discipline and humility to learn wisdom. So if you're going to pay attention to wisdom, then you must resolve to be a strange bird. You must learn a new way of fighting, utterly foreign to your fellow citizens.

Whatever funny names you might be called, it will be worth it. If you pay attention to wisdom, you will be preserved. You will be the one preserving truth. You will know, while others mock and jeer. There will be hope for the world because you will be a guardian of truth in a vast desert of lies.

But we are not only to pay attention to wisdom. We must also pay attention to the strange woman's ways. The father does not want his son to be ignorant concerning her. How many children have been fed to the wolves because parents did not school them in the ways of wolves?

A wise father says to beware of her temptations. "For the lips of a forbidden woman drip honey, and her speech is smoother than oil" (Proverbs 5:3). We long for the day when we won't have to put up with her lying lips. But you will have to turn a deaf ear to her as long as you walk in this world. This father references the sweetest and smoothest substances known to ancient Israel, which tell us she is particularly good at tempting her prey. Her appeal is not merely to the outer man but the inner man. With her words, she will caress your ego. She will appeal to your distorted, fleshly masculinity. She will season her poisonous lie with sweet truths.

We must pay attention to the truth about her. She is painfully bitter. She is said to be as bitter as wormwood—a plant so bitter it was used to ward off maggots and moths. She will leave you suffering in unbearable pain. Like a two-edged sword, she will cut into pieces your marriage, your manhood, and your faith.

Pay attention to the strange woman's ways: she walks toward death (Proverbs 5:5). She will not only leave you sick in body and soul, she will leave you dead. You might think, "I can recover from a stomachache. I can patch together the pieces once she has cut my character in two." The father says, "Beware of those lies, my son. There is no coming back from her destruction."

We will also be helped by paying attention to her ignorance. "She does not ponder the path of life; her ways wander, and she does not know it" (Proverbs 5:6). The strange woman is lost. She certainly cannot lead you to life because she does not know where she is going. The adulteress is a lost soul. "My son," says the father, "know the way of life. You ought to pity this poor woman. If you use her, you abuse her. You throw her into greater confusion. You throw her to hell."

We can be spared if we pay attention to the truth. We must fix our eyes and hearts on what is going on in this sexually sick world. So many lies abound about the topic of sex that you might think, "Where in the world do I start?" Begin with the truth of Scripture. God is not shy about teaching on this topic. Think and speak about His Word honestly in your homes. As you do so, the plethora of deceptions will become apparent, and you can steer clear of them.

AVOID THE STRANGE WOMAN

After hearing the call to pay attention, we must know what to avoid. And what we are to avoid is the strange woman.

A good father wants his son to know that avoiding the strange woman requires staying with wisdom. "And now, O sons, listen to me, and *do not depart* from the words of my mouth" (Proverbs 5:7). Having told them to pay attention to instruction, he now tells them to maintain it, to keep it. Now that you have it, do not let it go. He knows that keeping away from the strange woman is an endurance race. If you fumble wisdom halfway down the field, you're going to be in trouble.

Avoiding the strange woman means staying far away from her. The fool thinks he can cheat death. He wants to get close to fire without being burned. One who lives this way is a prideful man. He disregards the way God has made the world. He thinks far too highly of himself. The humble man does not test God.

Enormous pressure is on the church today to adopt a minimalistic approach to God's law. Here's what is happening. Imagine the son replying to his father, "But Dad, aren't I simply not to engage in intercourse with this adulteress? It seems a bit legalistic of you to tell me to stay away from her house. What's with all this adding to God's commandments?" Many Christians are tempted to respond to that inquiry with "Well, son, you're right. Technically only the adulterous act is wrong, so forgive me for my pharisaical ways, and go along wherever you want, I suppose."

That reply is problematic. It allows the loving and wise God behind the commandment to be killed, leaving only a meaningless rule. In other words, the son is the one being the Pharisee. A better response Christians must winsomely and boldly advance is this: "God, who has given you His good commandments, loves you. The further you are away from worshiping idols, the closer you'll be to God. The further you are away from stealing, the richer you will be. The further you are away from murder, the more life you will have. The further you are away from lying, the more truth you will understand. The further you are away from the adulteress, the more sexual pleasure you will enjoy in marriage. Now tell me again why you want to go close to her house?"

If we fail to stay away from the strange woman, we will forfeit our honor. A world of difference exists between wanting to have honor and wanting to be honored. It is the difference between wanting to do what is honorable and wanting to be recognized for it by others. We are not arrogant because we acknowledge honor is a precious thing. May every one of us, who takes the name of Christ, die with honor. May we finish the race set before us without bringing shame upon ourselves or, more importantly, upon our Christ.

We must avoid the strange woman, or we will lose our labor—"Lest strangers take their fill of your strength, and your labors go to the house of a foreigner" (Proverbs 5:10). How easily our high towers can be torn down by sexual immorality. Christians work hard to build a strong faith. We labor to build a healthy church and family. We toil diligently to store up treasure in heaven. We work to build character and credibility with our spouse, children, and fellow Christians. All that work! May this strike healthy fear into our hearts. Do you know how long and hard you have worked for these good things? Call to mind the blood and sweat, the emotional energy, the early morning prayers, the catechizing of children, the hours spent in service to the church. Could we truly spoil all that for which we have labored? We will not only lose our labors but embolden unbelievers to sin. The strength goes to foreigners. Paul writes of this in the New Testament, saying, "The name of God is blasphemed among the Gentiles because of you" (Romans 2:24).

If we do not avoid the strange woman, we will suffer in regret. We will groan and be consumed at the end of our lives. There, in our pain, we will lament that we did not listen to wise instruction. "How I hated discipline, and my heart despised reproof! I did not listen to the voice of my teachers or incline my ear to my instructors. I am at the brink of utter ruin in the assembled congregation" (Proverbs 5:12–14).

Let God's honest instruction here promote honest examination and conversation. If you are married, have an honest conversation about these things. Although this text focuses on a father's counsel to a son, plenty of honey-lipped men are out there who similarly tempt Christian women. Husbands and wives, take a hard look at what could be lost if you don't avoid sexual sin. Pray for one another. Reassure one another that you will avoid sexual immorality together. If you are a single man, find other godly men to be honest with. If you're a single woman, find other godly women, and talk over these matters.

EMBRACE YOUR WIFE

If he would avoid the sexual sin that kills, then a man must embrace his wife. He should do so because she is his permanent source of satisfaction. "Drink water from your own cistern, flowing water from your own well" (Proverbs 5:15). This well is a picture of a wife. A well supplies a home with satisfying water. Likewise, a wife supplies her husband with satisfying sexual love. It is significant that the picture is one of a well and not merely a vessel or a cup. The wife is not a paper cup to be used and discarded. She is the well-water system. She is the *very source* of sexual love and satisfaction for her husband. Ask yourself how valuable the water source for your home is. Without it, you die. Then you will know how noble the wife is as the permanent source of satisfaction for her husband.

Moreover, embrace your wife because spending your sexual love on other women is a defiling waste. "Should your springs be scattered abroad, streams of water in the streets?" (Proverbs 5:16). The picture is one of a precious resource ruined. When a spouse goes astray, the intimate passion once enjoyed in the marriage union is spilled out in the filthy streets. One of the most precious gifts God has given has been scattered on polluted street corners. Hebrews 13:4 says, "Let the marriage bed be undefiled." This is no arbitrary rule. It is the wisdom of God. He wants his children to know the joy of going to an undefiled marriage bed in covenant love.

The father says to embrace your wife. In marriage, you are now one with your spouse in an exclusive sexual union. "Let them be for yourself alone, and not for strangers with you" (Proverbs 5:17). These waters of intimate love are not for foreigners. These waters are to be enjoyed by husband and wife, best friends in covenant with each other before God. Christ says in Mark 10:7–8, "Therefore a man shall leave his father and mother and hold fast to his wife, and *the two shall become one flesh*. So they are no longer two but one flesh."

Embracing your wife includes rejoicing in her. You should be happy in your wife. Proverbs 18:22 says, "He who finds a wife finds a good thing and obtains favor from the LORD." Men, can you even begin to measure the gratitude we should have for our wives? Can you imagine that God, our creator, could give such a precious gift to us? She is handcrafted by God as a helper fit for you.

A part of that rejoicing includes being intoxicated always in her love. "A lovely deer, a graceful doe. Let her breasts fill you at all times with delight; be intoxicated always in her love" (Proverbs 5:19). The Bible forbids drunkenness and commands drunkenness. It forbids being drunk with wine and requires that a man be drunk in the love of his wife. He is not only to be intoxicated every now and then but *always*.

The son is encouraged to embrace his wife because embracing an adulteress is stupid. "Why should you be intoxicated, my son, with a forbidden woman and embrace the bosom of an adulteress?" (Proverbs 5:20). The answer is that there is absolutely no reason why. It is a senseless thing to do. She cannot provide satisfaction but only a bitter death. A God-given remedy to our sexually polluted age is the regular enjoyment of the undefiled marriage bed.

Fear God

If we would not be killed by sexual sin, then we must heed one final instruction. We have been urged to pay attention, avoid the strange woman, and embrace our wives. Finally, we must fear God.

Why should we? "For a man's ways are before the eyes of the LORD, and he ponders all his paths" (Proverbs 5:21). We should fear God because He sees all. How would we live if we really believed this? Have you noticed how self-controlled we can be when the eyes of others are on us? The presence of a little child with us can radically change our demeanor. It is quite convicting to think of how much a child's eye transforms us yet how little God's eye does. He is much more observant than a child. He sees us at every moment. We may simply need to confess that we have not appropriately feared Him and ask Him to help us fear Him more. Ask God to make you more aware of His presence with you. When sexual temptation comes, you will be far better off knowing the Lord is with you with eyes wide open.

Fear God because folly leads to death. There are only two options before us. Many want to claim that there is a middle way. But Scripture and human reason make plain that the choice is either the fear of God or folly. If you are fearing God, you are no fool. But if you are a fool, then you don't fear God.

The world mocks God's ways at every turn, especially when it comes to His wisdom regarding sex. But this topic sheds light on the fact that there are only two roads before us. The world says from one direction, "Do this and live." God says from the other, "No, do this and live." Mark the goodness of God's ways. No one wants a spouse to be unfaithful. The world's wisdom says that is a good idea. God's wisdom says that kind of thing leads to death. There is a man who has been perfectly faithful to His bride, and His name is Jesus Christ. He came into this world to save sinners. Even though we were unfaithful to Him and went after a stranger, because of His great love for us He came after us and brought us back to Himself. He did this through His perfect life, death, and resurrection. He washes His bride clean with His perfect righteousness.

6

A ROD FOR THE BACK OF FOOLS

Right thoughts about God are essential. If we think wrong thoughts about Him, we not only dishonor Him but harm ourselves. How many have suffered in this life and the life to come by embracing false notions about God? It is not easy to maintain true thoughts about our Creator today. He is often misrepresented. Many stagger in the dark, unable to come to a knowledge of the truth. Even those who have come to know the truth about God can drift ever so slowly from it if they fail to keep watch.

An often-neglected fundamental truth about God is that God hates. Modern man struggles with such a notion. But that is an indictment against us, not God. We have come to see love as a universal positive and hate as a universal negative. But what if you love harming others and hate when poor children are clothed? We need to recover the goodness of appropriate hate.

God displays His hatred of the wicked by judging them swiftly. God not only has anger but He has demonstrated that anger in the operation of His world.

GOD HATES THE WICKED

God hates the wicked. Many people are uncomfortable with this truth, but God teaches this plainly in many places. His wrath should sober us, but we should not despise Him for His righteous anger. Instead, we should stand in awe of how perfect, right, and beautiful God is in His wrath. The wise father says to his son, "There are six things that the LORD hates, seven that are an abomination to him" (Proverbs 6:16). Then he goes on to list wicked deeds the Lord despises.

First, the Lord hates pride. He hates "haughty eyes" (Proverbs 6:17). Man has had haughty eyes ever since Adam and Eve sinned against God. It is no surprise that there, at sin's inception, the Serpent tempted Adam and Eve with being "like God." Eve saw that the tree was "a delight to the eyes, and that the tree was to be desired to make one wise" (Genesis 3:6). We are prideful when we think higher of ourselves than we ought. We are prideful when we claim that there is nothing we are not worthy of. When, truly, there are innumerable things we are not worthy of. We are dust, and to dust we shall return. Pride is so pervasive among us that we have simply become accustomed to this sin. What a danger it is to us since it blends into our daily experience. Why is it such a great evil? Jonathan Edwards has said that pride "is God's most stubborn enemy!"[2]

The Lord also hates "a lying tongue" (Proverbs 6:17). This sin is particularly smooth at pretending like it is not a big one. We call them "little white lies" as if they are somehow okay. But God abhors the lying tongue. Why? The lying tongue speaks against His truth. We must become better at seeing that our sin is not only horizontal but vertical. We sin against God. It is His truth we distort when we speak lies. Psalm 5:6 says, "You destroy those who speak lies." God is zealous for His truth. He will not permit anyone to corrupt it.

The father continues by showing that the Lord hates "hands that shed innocent blood" (Proverbs 6:17). Right after Adam and Eve sinned, we see this sin come into the world as Cain murders his brother Abel. None of us can point our finger at Cain for, as the apostle Paul tells us in Romans 3:15, every one of us has "feet [that] are swift to shed blood." Jesus Himself tells us what is involved in the sixth commandment. He says in Matthew 5:21–22, "You have heard that it was said to those of old, 'You shall not murder, and whoever murders will be liable to judgment.' But I say to you that everyone who is angry with his brother will be liable to judgment; whoever insults his brother will be liable to the council; and whoever says, 'You fool!' will be liable to the hell of fire." God abhors murder. He is right to abhor it for in murder we slay people created in His image.

The Lord also hates "a heart that devises wicked plans" (Proverbs 6:18). Even before a sinful action is committed, even when the wickedness is simply in the planning stages, God hates it. Indeed, the heart of man is deceitful above all things. We not only do wickedness but delight in wickedness. And God hates this sinful desire in the heart. Some claim that a mere desire or orientation for sexual immorality is not wrong. They claim only the action is sinful. But this text says the wicked plan in the heart is something God hates. Our Lord in Matthew 5:27–28 says, "You have heard that it was said, 'You shall not commit adultery.' But I say to you that everyone who looks at a woman with lustful intent has already committed adultery with her in his heart."

The Lord also abominates "feet that make haste to run to evil" (Proverbs 6:18). The type of sin in view is sin without restraint. This sinner is going after sin without breaks. The Bible calls this debauchery. Sodom and Gomorrah is a clear picture of a society marked by a reckless pursuit of sin. They were so prideful that the men of the town almost beat a door down to homosexually assault those inside. Our danger is to think that our society is different, when, in fact, we are debauched to the core. God abhors those who cast off the fear of God and recklessly pursue sin.

The wise father tells his son that the Lord hates "a false witness who breathes out lies" (Proverbs 6:19). Having already noted God's hatred of the lying tongue, he adds here the Lord's displeasure when that lying tongue targets others. We are guilty of bearing false witness when we lie about another person. This sin happens not only when we flatly contradict the truth but also when we exaggerate another person's words or actions. One spouse says to another in an argument, "You *always* act this way!"

Well, unless the other spouse never sleeps, this is bearing false witness. "Oh, you know what I mean," comes the response. But such talk is merely justifying our hasty words, the lie that we have breathed out. We should be careful and accurate with our words for the Lord hates a false witness.

The last sin identified that the Lord hates is that of sowing discord among brothers (Proverbs 6:19). Sometimes, in a fallen world, a division is necessary. At times, when the truth is spoken, a separation will result. Jesus Himself came with a sword, setting a man against his family members. What is in view here is the dividing of God's children by deceitful schemes and lies. God loves His children and has wrath toward those who sinfully divide them.

GOD'S HATRED REVEALED

God not only hates the wicked but He has revealed this hatred to us in the world. The wise father wants his son's eyes open to the wrath of God displayed around Him. If the son has this knowledge, then he can avoid God's displeasure and walk in His blessing. We see His hatred in the swift judgment of God upon three types of sinners: the foolish talker, the sluggard, and the crooked man.

Judgment of the Foolish Talker

God displays His wrath in the trap He brings quickly upon the foolish talker. The father warns about putting up security for a stranger and becoming ensnared in our words (Proverbs 6:1–2). The specific foolishness involved here is becoming liable for someone's debt. But not only do we get caught in our words financially, we also get ensnared in our words when we agree to do something we are unable to do. Time passes, the person naturally expects that we will fulfill our promise, but we are caught in our words. We get caught in our words when we tell others we have done something that we have not done. In such situations, we "have come into the hand of [our] neighbor" (Proverbs 6:3). The bank will come for the money we promised. The friend will come for the action we promised.

Such coming into the hand of our neighbor is a sign of God's displeasure toward the foolish talker. It is the swift trap of God's judgment. The wise father knows this trap comes quickly. He counsels his son saying, "Then do this, my son, and save yourself, for you have come into the hand of your neighbor: go, hasten, and plead urgently with your neighbor. Give your eyes no sleep and your eyelids no slumber, save yourself like a gazelle from the hand of the hunter, like a bird from the hand of the fowler" (Proverbs 6:3–5). Do you sense the intensity of the situation? The one who is trapped in his words is in a very precarious position. He is like a trapped gazelle or bird soon to die at the hand of the hunter. The truth has a way of being found out, and so do foolish talkers.

So, we should heed the counsel of the wise father. If you are caught in your words, then go quickly to your neighbor, humble yourself, and do whatever is necessary to make things right, freeing yourself.

Judgment of the Sluggard

God's wrath is displayed not only in the trap He brings upon the foolish talker but also in the poverty He quickly brings upon the sluggard.

The sluggard is a lazy man. He is the opposite of the ant. He should study the ant and get wise. The ant goes through the seasons of work, preparing and gathering (Proverbs 6:8). In the same way, man should sow and then reap. But the lazy person lies in bed. The ant works without supervision, without a boss constantly directing and motivating (Proverbs 6:7). But the lazy person must routinely be told to get up and get going. Such laziness is a great evil in God's sight.

God displays His anger toward laziness by swiftly bringing poverty upon the sluggard—"A little sleep, a little slumber, a little folding of the hands to rest, and poverty will come upon you like a robber, and want like an armed man" (Proverbs 6:10–11). God's great displeasure with those who will not work diligently is seen in that it only takes a little sloth to bring about the judgment. It is only a "little sleep" and a "little folding of the hands" that results in poverty. The poverty itself does not ask for permission from the sluggard before coming upon him. The lack comes upon the sluggard like an armed man or a robber—poverty attacks with vehemence when a man gives in to laziness.

If we would simply open our eyes, we would see God's displeasure toward the wicked all around us. The truth cracks down on the foolish talker like a hunter upon his prey. Poverty assaults the sluggard like a thief in the night.

Judgment of the Crooked Man

And yet another example of God's wrath is seen in the calamity that so quickly comes upon the crooked man. Such a man is worthless, wicked, and crooked in speech (Proverbs 6:12). He "winks with his eyes, signals with his feet, points with his finger, with perverted heart devises evil, continually sowing discord" (Proverbs 6:13–14). This third character is a man living contrary to God and His holy law. He does not like the straight way but that of perversion. His distorted heart manifests itself in his sneaky and corrupt ways.

What is the result for such a crooked man? Calamity. "Therefore calamity will come upon him suddenly; in a moment he will be broken beyond healing" (Proverbs 6:15). God's wrath is displayed against this man by a terrible judgment. Not only is he trapped like the foolish talker, not only is he impoverished like the sluggard, but he is completely undone. He is broken entirely past the point of recovery. Like the other judgments, judgment comes "suddenly" and "in a moment" (Proverbs 6:15).

Living in Light of God's Wrath Revealed

We have seen that God displays His hatred of the wicked by judging them swiftly. The wise father wants his son to notice God's wrath revealed against ungodliness so he can live wisely in relationship to God in this world. As followers of Christ, we should do the same. So we must ask, since God displays His hatred of the wicked, how should we then live?

First, we should adjust our thoughts about God to what He has truly revealed concerning Himself. If God has told us in His Word and in His creation that He hates the wicked, then we should think of Him as hating the wicked. Do you think of God as being angry with the wicked every day? Are your prayers marked with acknowledgments of His wrath stored up against the ungodly? Has your awareness of God's wrath caused you to lament the false notions of Him that are so prevalent? Do you think of sinners as being in the hand of an angry God?

Similarly, we can count it a blessing to know what displeases God. God would be entirely just to leave us in the dark about what pleases and displeases Him. Having sinned so much against Him, we do not deserve to know this truth about Him. Think about how inconsistent we are with our anger in our relationships. We can come home and become angry with loved ones for no good reason. One day a friend's knock on our door may be met with a smile, and the next day, due to our circumstances, we may greet them in anger. It is not so with God. There is no guesswork. If we would avoid His displeasure, then we know what we must avoid wickedness.

Third, seeing that God has displayed His wrath, we should examine how we represent Him to others. Are you representing God truly? Are you teaching others about His wrath toward sin? We do this not only with our formal teaching but also informally by the things we approve and how we live each day. Our children know "Jesus loves me, this I know." And may they sing it every day! But do they sing of His wrath as well? May they also worship in song with "His chariots of wrath the deep thunderclouds form, and dark is His path on the wings of the storm." In the Puritan era, it was common to hear men recount hearing their mother's prayers for them when they were young. They remembered their mother's pleas to God that He would spare her little ones from the wrath to come. Do such appeals mark our prayers for our children, for our neighbors?

Fourth, seeing God's hatred displayed, our reverence, fear, and desire to please Him ought to increase. Surely, if we knew His wrath as it truly is, we would cover our mouths as Isaiah did saying, "Woe is me! For I am lost; for I am a man of unclean lips, and I dwell in the midst of a people of unclean lips!" (Isaiah 6:5). Could it be that one reason we are so flippant with God is that we have neglected this truth of His wrath against the wicked? We should make it our prayer that He fan into flame a deep and abiding reverence for Him.

Also, we should not only cultivate a sense of reverence at a heart level but we should be diligent in avoiding foolish talk, laziness, and crooked ways. God's wrath revealed should motivate us to strict obedience to all of God's commands. He hates foolish speech; we should be slow to speak and careful when we do. He hates the sluggard; we should work each day with all our strength. He hates the crooked man; we should set ourselves to study God's law and examine our lives by it. When times get tough, we must avoid any attempt to cheat God's ways to make things easier for ourselves.

Seeing God's wrath revealed against the wicked, our concern for the lost must increase. What a swift judgment He brings upon the ungodly! And how severe His wrath will be. The lost sinner will be broken beyond healing at the day of judgment. When is the last time your heart broke for the unbeliever? Let us follow our Master, praying, "Father forgive them for they know not what they do." A genuine awareness of the wrath of God will not leave your heart unmoved for your lost neighbor. You will not *merely* say, even if true, "He gets only what He deserves in God's wrath." The Christian, having a sense of God's wrath, cries out with compassion, "Flee! Flee the wrath to come!"

Seventh, our love for Christ must be inflamed by this truth. Seeing God's swift judgment must stir our love for Christ. He was made sin for us and suffered God's terrible judgment in our place. This chapter has addressed a wrath that believers will never know because Christ has known it for us. Christ was trapped by our words. He was impoverished by our laziness. He was broken by our crookedness. What do you see in the cross but the wrath of God displayed. Hallelujah, that it is not only wrath displayed there. Mercy and judgment are what you find in the cross. May we love Christ more, seeing what He has suffered for us.

Perhaps you hear this truth of God's wrath and think it is just too much or too heavy-handed. Charles Spurgeon, a nineteenth-century preacher, once responded to such a thought by saying, "If there be a man before me who says that the wrath of God is too heavy a punishment for his little sin, I ask him, if the sin be little, why does he not give it up?"

7

EMBRACE WISDOM, NOT THE SEDUCTRESS

We live amid rampant sexual immorality. Surely sexual immorality has been around since sin entered the world. But we live in an uptick, in cataclysmic sexually perverse times. This point really does not need proving.

The sexual revolution was a social movement from the 1960s to the 1980s that eradicated traditional sexual behavior. This so-called sexual liberation—which is actually sexual slavery—included the acceptance of sex outside of marriage. Several things came in the wake of this sexual revolution: the normalization of contraception, public nudity, pornography, premarital sex, homosexuality, alternative forms of sexuality, no-fault divorce, and the legalization of abortion.

We are now fifty years on the far side of that sexual revolution. We have same-sex marriage as the law of our land and seventy-one gender options on Facebook. We have judges removing a young girl from her parents' custody because they would not let her undergo hormone treatments to make her more manlike.[3]

What's the point in identifying our sexual corruption? It is to see how easily we can succumb to this sexual perversion. We don't get to look at

53

these outlandish abominations and say, "I've really got my sexual ethic in shape." No, we need to see that from the moment we were born we have been breathing in these toxins. If there is a flood out there, you are more likely to have water in your house. In times like these, even good people get seduced by the seductress, often unknowingly. Our cultural norms, accepted by almost everyone, are patterns built on sexual corruption.

To put it bluntly, sexual suicide is in the streets, so board up your windows and bar the door. A sexual plague of death is among us, so run for your life. In this chapter, we are going to see just how to do that—how to live amid deadly sexual corruption. We will hear the wise words of a loving father to his son, as he admonishes his son to get wisdom and get away from the seductress.

The essential point is this: If you want to live, embrace wisdom, not the seductress. It is impossible to embrace both wisdom and the seductress. Wisdom and the seductress are like oil and water. They don't mix. They are like hot and cold. You cannot get them together. The fool and the seductress go hand in hand. They are best buds. On the other side of town, wisdom and sexual purity walk together. The seductress leads the fool to her house, which is where folks go to die. In contrast, wisdom leads her companions to her home, which is full of life and good things.

KEEP TO THE COMMANDMENT

If you want to live, keep to the commandment (Proverbs 6:20–24). It is essential to see that such an exhortation comes from a father speaking to his son. The son did not become his father's son by keeping the commandment. Sonship was given to the son freely. In the same way, Christians become the Father's children by free grace. We have not earned our place in His home. But now, the Father addresses us as his blood-bought children, saying, "If you want life and blessing, keep to the commandment." The father employs a variety of terms for *commandment* here, all of which have the idea of God's law and truth.

He says to keep to the commandment of your father and mother (Proverbs 6:20). How striking is it that the first appeal designed to help you resist the strong pull of sexual immorality is "Listen to your parents"? Pay attention to your mother's law. Little boys who won't happily and swiftly obey their mothers will soon be in the prostitute's bed. It is no surprise that rebellion against parents has come with our sexual corruption. Do you see the connection? In 1988 there was a popular song lamenting parental authority called *Parents Just Don't Understand*. Thirty years later, the teens who sang the anthem have grown up to be judges who remove young girls from their parents' homes because they won't let them try to become boys.[4] In kindness, God brings each one of us into the world, telling us to keep the commandments of people we did not choose. We are sexually polluted because we don't like being told what to do. If we humble ourselves before God's authority expressed through faithful parents, then we will live.

The father continues, instructing, "Keep to the commandment, always." He says, "Bind them on your heart always; tie them around your neck" (Proverbs 6:21). The father says to his son, "Take my commandments with you wherever you go. Do not discard the commandment when you leave home." How easy it is to be sobered by God's Word in one moment and negligent of it in the next. The enemy will happily let you drink in the truth for a moment if he can expel it from your system later. Keeping to the commandment is an endurance race. It calls for perseverance and continual remembrance. If you keep commandments close only some of the time, then you won't live. You will fall prey to the seductress.

The father again advises his son to keep to the commandment for it gives direction—"When you walk, they will lead you; when you lie down, they will watch over you; and when you awake, they will talk with you" (Proverbs 6:22). God's commands will guide the son through various times in his life. Life is going to happen one way or the other. You do not get to hit pause on this one. Situations will arise where you are going to be caught in a trap if you lack God's commandments. If the son does not keep to God's commandment, then he will be lost as he walks, attacked when he sleeps, and ignorant when he wakes.

The father wants his son to keep to the commandment even when it corrects him. He says, "For the commandment is a lamp and the teaching a light, and the reproofs of discipline are the way of life" (Proverbs 6:23). How tempting it is to throw away the commandment when it corrects us. We love the words that confirm what we are doing. We keep to the uplifting encouragement. But when reproof comes, we find ways to disregard it. When discipline comes, we try to avoid it. But "whoever loves discipline loves knowledge, but he who hates reproof is stupid" (Proverbs 12:1).

The father shows there is a purpose in keeping to the commandment. Doing so will help "to preserve you from the evil woman, from the smooth tongue of the adulteress" (Proverbs 6:24). The son needs an antidote to this woman's advances. He needs a life-preserver from her flattery. That preserver is God's teaching. If the son keeps to it, he will be protected from the seductress.

If keeping to the commandment is the way to life, then some questions follow. Are you holding to God's commandment? Are you happy God has given you authorities? Do you welcome correction?

Love Not the Seductress

The father continues by telling his son not to love the seductress. He aims for the son's affections.

It is challenging not to love the seductress. The father warns, "Do not desire her beauty in your heart, and do not let her capture you with her eyelashes" (Proverbs 6:25). This evil woman is a temptress, and all temptations present sin as satisfying. Sin presents itself as something beautiful when, in truth, it seeks to capture you. Don't be deceived. Prepare your heart for her advances. The father's counsel is worth modeling in our own parenting. We don't do our sons any favors by leaving them ignorant to temptation. We must warn ourselves, and each other, about temptation, exposing the lies of the enemy.

The father points out that the seductress will viciously impoverish your life. He tells his son the ugly truth about the seductress—"for the price of a prostitute is only a loaf of bread, but a married woman hunts down a precious life" (Proverbs 6:26). The prostitute will leave you with nothing but a loaf of bread. The married woman is a woman married to someone else; she is an adulteress. What does she do? She hunts down others and kills them. This woman will leave you destitute and dead. The true woman nurtures. She is a life-giver. The true woman helps and builds up. But not this evil woman.

The father says the son should not love the seductress, and for good reason. Punishment is inescapable for those who do. He marks the inevitable punishment for those who commit adultery. If you carry fire near your chest, you will be burned. If you walk on hot coals, your feet will be scorched (Proverbs 6:27–28). The truth is sobering—"none who touches her will go unpunished" (Proverbs 6:29). How insane is this reoccurring experience of mankind? We think we can sin and get away with it. We believe we can cheat God's universal law. But you can no more sin and escape punishment than you can place your hand on a hot stove and not be burned! The devil has been lying about this from the beginning. He said to Eve, "God said you would die if you eat, but you will not surely die." He was wrong. And the voice inside your head about cheating sexual sin's punishment is wrong too.

After noting the certainty of the punishment, the father highlights the gravity of it. A man who commits adultery "destroys himself" (Proverbs 6:32). The jealousy of the offended husband makes him furious (Proverbs 6:34). The particular destruction in view is dishonor. No one despises the thief if he steals to satisfy his hunger. Yes, the thief will be punished, and he will have to pay and even lose all the goods of his house. But the severity of the adulterer's punishment is much greater—"He will get wounds and dishonor" (Proverbs 6:33).

The pain that accompanies the embrace of the seductress is long-lasting—"his disgrace will not be wiped away" (Proverbs 6:33). The enraged man "will not spare when he takes revenge," and neither will he accept compensation (Proverbs 6:34–35). Sexual immorality is terribly costly because it results in consequences that stay around for a long time. Every sin is wicked in God's sight, but they are not all equally wicked. All sin will harm you. But some stings burn longer than others. Love not the seductress. Keep your heart from going out to her because she will bring you bitter pain that won't go away anytime soon.

How are we to respond to the wise father's counsel? We need to speak more plainly about the seductress and the punishment that goes with her. Point out the punishment of the sexually immoral. What a wicked thing we have done giving into political correctness. What a terrible thing we have done letting others tell us what we can say and how we can speak. We have left many suffering the severe, lasting wounds of the seductress. How many would have repented of their corrupt desires if we had told them before what would happen to them?

Oh, the wrath we will face if we say that the scantily clad woman on Instagram wants to kill you. Yet that is precisely what God has said in His Word.

Young women, don't take fashion tips from this strange woman. She is no true woman. She is not a life-giving woman. She is not doing what God created women to do. Why would you want your pants or lipstick color to match *hers*?

Older women, tell your sons to love not the strange woman. Set an example for them of a nurturing, godly woman so that they can quickly identify the fraud.

Young men and old, do not love this loveless woman. Fathers, tell your sons what happens to those who do. Sons, pay attention, or else be burned with enduring disgrace.

LOVE WISDOM

The father told the son at the outset that he must keep to wisdom. But now he drives his exhortation deeper. The son must not only keep to wisdom, he must love wisdom. Strict adherence to the Word of God alone will not do. A cold heart can memorize the Father's commands all it wants, but such a heart is still susceptible to the seductress. The father identifies how we are to love wisdom.

In love for wisdom, store up God's commands like a precious treasure—"treasure up my commands with you" (Proverbs 7:1). The father wants his son to treat faithful teaching like riches. The son is to hide away

God's truth so that it will be protected. You can love wisdom enough to get it but fail to love it enough to keep it. We guard what we love. If we were given $10,000 cash, we would have a plan in place for how to store up and protect that money. But money is not the only thing in need of protection; God's teaching is continuously under assault. Those who love His teaching will defend it. Sadly, it is all too common to see a faithful Christian correct one who has distorted God's truth, only to have other believers upset with the faithful Christian for speaking a word of correction. What is the cause of this? We do not love God's wisdom like precious treasure. We are not concerned about storing it up and guarding it.

In love for wisdom, prize God's Word above everything else—"keep my teaching as the apple of your eye" (Proverbs 7:2). We esteem the apple of our eye above all else. Yet it is easy to drift from our love of Scripture. What a foolish thing it is when we do. The father tells us to love what is lovable. If we were thinking rightly, we would say with the psalmist, "Oh how I love your law!" (Psalm 119:97). His Word is "perfect, reviving the soul; . . . sure, making wise the simple; . . . right, rejoicing the heart; . . . pure, enlightening the eyes; . . . true, and righteous altogether. More to be desired are they than gold" (Psalm 19:7–10). How could the Father's teaching not be the apple of our eye?

In love for wisdom, let continual study engrave God's instruction on your heart—"bind them on your fingers; write them on the tablet of your heart" (Proverbs 7:3). If they are on your fingers, then they are always with you for continual study. If they are written on your heart, then they have been internalized. His commands are now working on your affections. The prophet Jeremiah tells us that this writing on the heart is a gift brought to Christians in the new covenant. We should ask the Spirit to work God's truth in us more deeply so we simply cannot think of any other way to live than by His commands.

In love for wisdom, establish a relationship with her as an intimate loved one—"Say to wisdom, 'You are my sister,' and call insight your intimate friend" (Proverbs 7:4). The son's relationship with wisdom must move beyond the theoretical and intellectual. He must love her so profoundly that the immoral woman becomes her competitor, a senseless enemy, and a threat to his covenant relationship with lady wisdom. We should stand against sexual immorality as a sworn enemy of our dearly loved one, lady wisdom. If the seductress increases, our lady wisdom decreases. If lady wisdom increases, the seductress decreases.

KEEP AWAY FROM THE SEDUCTRESS

In the beginning, the father said to *keep to* the commandment. Now he says to *keep away* from the seductress. This action is the kind a man takes if he wants to live.

He says to keep away from the seductress for only fools go near her. The father recounts looking out of the window of his house (Proverbs 7:6–9). What has he seen? He has seen the simple young fool. What is the simple young fool doing? He's passing near the home of the seductress. When is he doing it? At night in the darkness. He's an ignorant guy doing an ignorant thing in an ignorant way. The father has told his son previously to avoid this strange woman. He has told his son not to go near her house. Here is an example of a fool doing so. The fool thinks he can get close to sin. The fool puts himself in situations he should never have been in.

The father explains that the seductress deserves to be avoided. He describes her ugliness (Proverbs 7:10–13). She is "dressed as a prostitute." She signals men by the way she dresses. She wants men's eyes on her. She wants to show them her sexual promiscuity. She is wily of heart. She is crafty or skilled at gaining an advantage. She is loud. She knows nothing of the "gentle and quiet spirit," which is very precious in God's sight (1 Peter 3:4). She is wayward. She's stubborn against God and His commandments. She's hardened in her crooked ways. Her feet do not stay at home. She is not satisfied with what God has given her. She is out and about always, coveting, looking for more than what is hers. She is covering every corner lying in wait for her prey. She's not one who hopes in the Lord like the holy women of old (1 Peter 3:5). She's not waiting on God to satisfy her desire. She seizes the fool, kisses him, and with bold face, speaks. The shock of such an encounter leaves the fool stupefied. But it shouldn't. We call to mind a thousand images of such a woman suddenly kissing a man like this. In our day, such action is passed with a chuckle and a shaking of the head. But it should not be. What wicked sin is on display? Her pride. Her "bold face"—that is, her impudent, shameless, defiant face. She has not done anything attractive. She has done an abomination. She has not done anything cute. She reversed God's good and right established order.

The father warns his son to keep away from the seductress for she persuades with seductive speech (Proverbs 7:14–21). She pretends that all is right between her and God. She has, after all, offered her sacrifices. She flatters the fool. She's come out just for him. She's sought him out diligently. She's now found just what she was looking for. She makes false promises of joy and passion and has taken great measures so they can delight themselves with sexual immorality. She overcomes his hesitations with false assurances, and she guarantees there will be no consequences, for her husband is on a long journey. Mark the tactics of the seductress. Note how many ways the truth can be manipulated, and keep away.

Finally, the father warns his son that this woman has taken many an ignorant fool to death (Proverbs 7:22–27). The fool goes like an ox to the slaughter, like a stag pierced in the liver by an arrow, or like a bird in a snare. The fool has been played. He does not know his actions will cost him his life. See the danger. You can honestly think, "I'm good," and can genuinely believe you have things under control, saying, "These words of warning don't apply to me." All your genuine feelings don't mean a thing. You're still dead.

So, what should you do? The father tells you, "And now, O sons, listen to me, and be attentive to the words of my mouth" (Proverbs 7:24). Pay attention to faithful teaching, not your own thoughts, however reasonable they seem to you. Why should you stay away from the seductress? Because "many a victim has she laid low, and all her slain are a mighty throng. Her house is the way to Sheol, going down to the chambers of death" (Proverbs 7:26–27).

If you want to live, embrace wisdom, not the seductress. That's the father's counsel to his son. Keep close to God's commandments. Love them!

Set your heart on God's truth, and ask Him to inflame your desire for His Word. While you do so, love not the seductress. Stay away from her! Flee sexual immorality. Get as far away as you can.

You have likely seen the terrible consequences of our sexual corruption. You have seen homes split apart. You have witnessed fatherless children and heartbreak. Could it be that God knows what He is doing when it comes to sex? Could it be that embracing wisdom—and not the seduction of sexual immorality—truly is the way to life?

If that's true, where do you find wisdom that you might embrace it? Scripture says that all the treasures of wisdom are found in a man named Jesus Christ. He is the Son of God. He became flesh two thousand years ago and lived a life of perfect obedience to God's law. He never embraced the seductress. He laid down His life on a cross to suffer God's judgment for sinners like you and me. He was put to disgrace. He was impoverished. He was wounded and went down to death. Why? He was perfect! He suffered that punishment in place of His people. He subbed in for them. He now has conquered death. He has risen again. He's alive today and able to save those who turn away from sin to Him.

You cannot clean yourself up from your impurity. The call is not for you to purify yourself from your sexual uncleanness so He will accept you. The call is for you to see that you're going to die for your sin and to call out to Jesus to save you. He is the purity. And He is yours through faith. Trust Him, the pure one, and He will cleanse you of all your sin. He will wash you and save you for all eternity. Embrace Christ, and you will embrace wisdom. You will live.

8

WISDOM: A BLESSED LADY

Romans 11:33 says, "Oh, the depth of the riches and wisdom and knowledge of God! How unsearchable are his judgments and how inscrutable his ways!" God's wisdom, the apostle Paul says, is beyond finding out. His wisdom is an infinitely deep well of riches. His wisdom is invaluable.

The fantastic thing then, the breathtaking good news, is that He would rain down His wisdom upon us. He will graciously extend His wisdom to us that we might live an abundant life in this world.

Why do we need to remember the richness of God's wisdom and His gracious extension of that wisdom to us? Two reasons come to mind. First, we are ridiculously foolish. Without Christ, we are all a bunch of bone-heads. Romans 3:11 backs me up on that. It says, "No one understands." Jesus, too, in John 15:5 says, "Apart from me you can do nothing." So, we're just a bunch of blockheaded simpletons without Jesus.

But on top of that, too often we are as enthusiastic about getting wisdom as grade-school kids are about getting broccoli for dinner. We are all too comfortable in our ignorance. It's like we enjoy groping around in the dark banging our knees on unseen objects. Our ignorance and indifference get us into all sorts of trouble. We're contented fools and the worse off for it.

But God is gracious, and He helps us in our trouble. He extends His Word to us with precious promises. He motivates us by showing us just how invaluable His wisdom is.

In this chapter, I want to highlight that the wisdom of God—which in reality is Christ—is metaphorically spoken of as a blessed lady crying out to mankind. As she speaks, we see just what a wonderful blessing God's wisdom is so that we might embrace this precious treasure.

Find wisdom, for she is a very blessed lady. That's the main idea before us. These are words that can woo us off the couch to the gates of wisdom. We see four different blessings of lady wisdom. Each one stirs us to find her. First, there are wisdom's blessed words. Second, wisdom's blessed possessions. Third, wisdom's blessed history. And finally, wisdom's blessed necessity.

WISDOM'S WORDS

God displays the glory of His wise words that we might pay attention to them.

Lady wisdom cries out to the children of man (Proverbs 8:1–5). "Does not wisdom call? Does not understanding raise her voice?" (Proverbs 8:1). This lady is not silent. She is speaking out. She's not bitterly hiding away, saying, "Let mankind find its own way." No, she's graciously raising her voice to the simple and foolish (Proverbs 8:5). Not only is she crying out but she's doing so "on the heights beside the way, [and] at the crossroads she takes her stand" (Proverbs 8:2). She has gone above and beyond to be heard. If passersby do not listen, it will surely not be her fault. As if they would not listen to her on the road, she has made her way to the gate of the town (Proverbs 8:3). Plainly demanding an audience, she speaks directly, saying, "To you, O men, I call" (Proverbs 8:4). What a picture of God's gracious calling out to this world! He speaks through His creation, for the heavens declare His glory and the skies above proclaim His handiwork (Psalm 19:1). He has also spoken through His Son, Jesus, who cried out to mankind during His earthly ministry. God has spoken through His prophets and apostles, His Holy Scriptures, which have been spread far and wide across this globe. God would be perfectly just not to utter a single Word to rebels like us, but He has spoken, not whispered, and declared good news to us like this lady raising her voice.

Not only does the blessed lady cry out but she also speaks noble words. Lady wisdom instructs, "Hear, for I will speak noble things, and from my lips will come what is right" (Proverbs 8:6). God's wise words are good. They are upright words. Paul says in Ephesians 4:29, "Let no corrupting talk come out of your mouths." Filthy words have no place in the people of God, for they have no place in God Himself. It is no surprise to see that Paul quickly follows his words in Ephesians with a call not to grieve the Holy Spirit. Surely the Holy Spirit is grieved by unholy talk, for He only speaks what is right. In this corrupt world, sometimes we can be baffled about how to live Christianly. Well, the noble words of God are the key. Psalm 119:9 says, "How can a young man keep his way pure? By guarding it according to your word."

The blessed lady not only speaks noble words but *true* words. Her words are full of both goodness and truth, "for my mouth will utter truth" and "all the words of my mouth are righteous; there is nothing twisted or crooked in them" (Proverbs 8:7–8). The one who understands her words sees the straightness of them. We face people asking the same question Pontius Pilate asked our Lord two thousand years ago, "What is truth?" What a scene! The Roman governor asks the truth Himself what truth is. People want to know reality. A desire for the truth is inescapable, even in our silly days when one person can claim, "You have your truth, and I have mine." Such a statement is a truth claim! Even those who pretend like they don't care about truth care about truth. Where can you find truth? In the wise words of God. Like this lady, He speaks perfectly accurate words; there are no errors in His Word.

The blessed lady also speaks valuable words. Her words are precious and beautiful. She says, "Take my instruction instead of silver . . . and gold" for wisdom is "better than jewels and all that you may desire cannot compare with her" (Proverbs 8:10–11). If you listen to wisdom, you will not only live an ethical and knowledgeable life, you will live a beautiful life. There is nothing you can desire—nothing at all—that compares with lady wisdom's words. Jewels are very precious things. They are rare. They appeal to our eyes. But the wisdom of God will make you richer than precious stones, silver, and gold. We are somewhat uncomfortable with saying some things are uglier than others, but some things are indeed uglier than others. Some lives are uglier than others because they have turned a deaf ear to the words of lady wisdom. Other lives shine with greater beauty and delight because they have listened diligently to God's wisdom.

Consider how blessed the words of wisdom are. Have you been listening to the call of God that steadily rings out through creation and Scripture? Have you been pursuing that which is most noble, true, and beautiful? Consider that some people will pay attention to the word of Christ and become truer, better, and more beautiful. Every day we are either making progress in these precious things or falling behind. Are you listening?

WISDOM'S POSSESSIONS

We see that wisdom not only has blessed words but she also has blessed possessions. Any young man pursuing a young lady should take note of her words. Does she speak words that build up? But he should also take note of what she possesses. Does she possess the fruit of the Spirit? Who are her friends? When you marry her, her possessions will become your possessions. So, wisdom's blessed possessions motivate us to find her.

First, we see lady wisdom possesses prudence (Proverbs 8:12). The idea is that she is shrewd. She has a canny ability to navigate the world in an advantageous way. In the Old Testament book of Joshua, we hear of the Israelites crossing the Jordan River and conquering the promised land. When the Gibeonites heard about this, Joshua 9:4 says they "acted with cunning." They took up worn-out sacks, put on worn-out clothes, and went to Joshua saying that they lived a long way off and wanted to make a peace agreement with the Israelites. Joshua made peace with them, only to find out later that they lived nearby and should have been conquered. The Gibeonites exercised prudence, and so will you if you find wisdom.

Lady wisdom also possesses the fear of the Lord (Proverbs 8:13). The fear of the Lord is defined as the hatred of evil, and lady wisdom says she has this hatred of evil. She's like the Proverbs 31 woman, of whom it is said, "A woman who fears the LORD is to be praised" (Proverbs 31:30). We've seen before in Proverbs that the fear of the Lord is a deep reverence for His majestic holiness. The person who has this reverence for the Lord hates all that is opposed to Him and His ways. Don't be confused on this point. Many think that the fear of the Lord means you don't hate anything. Some say that if you fear the Lord, well then, you won't get angry. But the opposite is true. If you fear the Lord, then you must hate certain things; you must get angry. Much of our broader culture says that every lifestyle is okay as long as it doesn't hurt anyone. The Christian must plainly reject that. And in rejecting that you will be seen as a narrow-minded bigot by the world. If believers shrink back when such accusations come, it is because they do not fear the Lord; they are not embracing lady wisdom. She hates evil and perverted speech, which is the fear of the Lord.

Lady wisdom not only possesses the fear of the Lord but she also has strength for ruling well. She says, "I have counsel and sound wisdom; I have insight; I have strength. By me kings reign, and rulers decree what is just; by me princes rule, and nobles, all who govern justly" (Proverbs 8:14–16). Every Christian has some responsibility to rule. Husbands lead in the home. Parents oversee children. Believers must manage responsibilities in the workplace. And each of us must rule over ourselves with self-control. Wisdom can help us rule well in all these areas. How hard it is to rule justly! Complex situations have a way of presenting themselves. But wisdom will supply what we need, and that is a real blessing, for a ruler without wisdom is a dangerous thing. There is a reason why we have such ungodly laws and so many unjust decrees: it is because many of our governing officials and the people who put them there are foolish. They lack wisdom. Without her, we will not govern justly.

This lady wisdom also possesses love for those who love her (Proverbs 8:17). She's a lady who will love you back, big time. It is interesting that wisdom is personified as a woman on this count. Generally, we can see this lovely quality in females. If someone loves them, they seem to return double the amount of love. They are like flowers that spring forth with beauty and a pleasant scent when the rain of love falls upon them. God's wisdom is like this. If we love His wisdom, His wisdom will love us back. His wise Word will redouble our efforts if we give ourselves to it. Here is encouragement if you have not attended to His Word as you ought. Remember that He does not require that you store up large amounts of time in His wisdom before experiencing His love. He's not like a hard, dry soil that must be labored over extensively only to get a few crops. He's a rich, dark soil that will produce abundant love for you if you will love His instruction.

Lady wisdom has another possession, and that is riches (Proverbs 8:18). She doesn't have fleeting wealth but enduring riches. Her "fruit is better than gold," and she grants an inheritance to those who love her (Proverbs 8:19, 21). There are connections between living wisely and flourishing. Financial wealth is not specifically in view here, although there are certainly wise principles of stewardship that generally lead to the financial fruit of those principles. But the primary sense here is that the one who gets wisdom will lead an enriched life, for she's a rich lady. Her fruit is even better than gold. She walks in the paths of righteousness and justice. So, the life lived on these paths is a rich life. Do you want to live exceedingly well? Then walk justly and uprightly. How can you do that? Find wisdom—she's the blessed lady who knows the way.

Seeing what lovely possessions wisdom has, how should we respond? We find encouragement here to *love lady wisdom.* Her blessed words compel us to listen to her. And her rich possessions move us to love her. Do you want to live shrewdly, fearing the Lord and hating evil? Then love wisdom. She will love you back. She will help you lead others and exercise self-control, leading you to walk with her down paths lined with gold.

WISDOM'S HISTORY

In addition to wisdom's blessed words and possession, she also has a blessed history. Her history is marked by her relationship to the Lord and the world of man. The mystery of this history is profound, pointing to Christ Himself as true wisdom who has always been with the Father, delighting with Him in creation.

Notice that wisdom was fathered by the Lord before His work of creation. "The LORD possessed [fathered] me at the beginning of his work, the first of his acts of old" (Proverbs 8:22). The relationship between the Lord and wisdom precedes the making of the world. For, "ages ago I was set up, at the first, before the beginning of the earth" (Proverbs 8:23). Again, "when there were no depths I was brought forth, when there were no springs abounding with water" (Proverbs 8:24). Wisdom was not only before the water but before the mountains, hills, fields, and dust (Proverbs 8:25–26). Wisdom here claims superiority over all that has been made. If we are ever going to learn how to live rightly in this created world, then we must find wisdom, which precedes anything and everything that has been made. You've heard the older man say to the younger, "Boy, I was around when you were just a twinkle in your daddy's eye." Here, wisdom says the same to us.

But wisdom was not only before the Lord's work of creation, wisdom was with the Lord as He created. Wisdom says, "When he established the heavens, I was there; when he drew a circle on the face of the deep" (Proverbs 8:27). Wisdom was with the Lord when He firmed up the skies and the foundations of the deep. Wisdom was with Him when the Lord shaped the sea, marking its limits, and designating how far the foundations of the earth would go (Proverbs 8:29). Wisdom is upping the ante on us. Wisdom says, "I've told you about my blessed words and possessions, but now hear this: I'm before you, O children of man. I was there when Yahweh put a stop to the swelling tides of the Atlantic Ocean. I was there at the outset. I watched the Lord pack down the ocean floor where the octopus runs and the sixgill shark swims."

Wisdom was with the Lord in this work, but in addition, wisdom worked with the Lord on the earth. Wisdom declares, "Then I was beside him, like a master workman" (Proverbs 8:30). The picture of Christ as true wisdom has been steadily growing clearer. Now that picture is revealed with great clarity. This wisdom is Christ, the master workman who labored with the Father in creation. John 1:1–3 says, "In the beginning was the Word, and the Word was with God, and the Word was God. He was in the beginning with God. All things were made through Him, and without Him was not any thing made that was made." Colossians 1:16 says of Christ, "For by him all things were created." The world was created with wisdom—God has fashioned a wisely designed world. Wisdom calls to us, then, saying, "You cannot live as you ought in this world without me! You cannot function in the world I created apart from me!"

As wisdom worked with the Lord, they rejoiced in each other and in their created world. What a history this is, for "I was beside him, like a master workman, and I was daily his delight, rejoicing before him always, rejoicing in his inhabited world and delighting in the children of man" (Proverbs 8:30–31). As the Father and Son went about their work, they were happy. After each day's work we hear that familiar refrain in Genesis, "And God saw that it was good." It was good, and He knew that it was good. He rejoiced in its goodness. He celebrated over the long neck of the giraffe. He laughed with glee over the flight of the hummingbirds. And then we hear these awe-inspiring words: He was "delighting in the children of man" (Proverbs 8:31). Wisdom and the Lord smiled upon mankind.

As we find wisdom, we also find delight. We live happily as we ought to live. We smile upon God in Christ, and He smiles back. We should find wisdom, for then we will be caught up into this happy relationship. We join Christ, who is wisdom, in a joyful relationship with the Lord. We go about the work of God in this inhabited world with gladness.

Seeing this marvelous history, stand in awe of wisdom. Stand in awe of the One who is wisdom—that is, Christ. He was with the Father at the beginning. He knows the work of creation inside and out. Through Him was everything made that was made. And He is a happy creator. Surely we have brought great sorrow upon ourselves through our sin. We have fallen away from our Creator and polluted His good world. But in Christ we have been made new; indeed He is making all things new. We should relish Christ our wisdom and happily join Him in His present work in this world.

WISDOM'S NECESSITY

Wisdom makes a final appeal to us that we might find her. We've seen her blessed words, possessions, and history. Now we see her blessed necessity. Her necessity means that she is the necessary thing. She is the decisive thing. She is that which everything hangs on.

How is this so? It is so because "whoever finds me finds life and obtains favor from the LORD" (Proverbs 8:35). There are many nice things to have that are not necessary to life. Some things are necessary to certain other things. You need transportation to go long distances. You may need glasses to see better. If you want to stay dry, you will need shelter. But what is plainly stated here is how we can get something far better. What is offered to us is life, and not just any life but a life of the Lord's favor. How do you get the pleasure of God, the smile of God upon you? Find wisdom.

But this truth cuts both ways; wisdom is the decisive thing. If you get her, you get a life of the Lord's favor. But if you don't get her, you die. Wisdom sobers us, warning, "But he who fails to find me injures himself; all who hate me love death" (8:36). You cannot claim middle ground. You love wisdom and get life, or else you hate her and love death. You cannot say, "Oh, I'm okay with wisdom but not all that into her." No, if you fail to find her, you will be severely injured. That's because wisdom is the decisive thing. She's an all-or-nothing lady.

What are we to do then? Wisdom encourages us in the right path, saying, "Blessed is the one who listens to me, watching daily at my gates, waiting beside my doors" (Proverbs 8:34). Watch daily at her gates. Find her. That's what we are to do. If we diligently seek God's wisdom, His truth, His Christ, then we will be very blessed people.

If you find you're not seeking wisdom diligently, if you're not listening to God's Word, or heeding the word of Christ, then you not only have an obedience problem, you have a belief problem. That's what this passage is all about. You really don't believe wisdom is a blessed lady. You doubt whether her words are really blessed, and you're not sure she really possesses the blessings she says she does. You're unsure about wisdom's awe-inspiring history and whether wisdom is the most crucial thing for you to live under the favor of God. So, the call is for you to believe God's Word. Take God at His word. Take Christ, who is wisdom, at His word. Trust that wisdom is all that God says it is, and you will find yourself waiting at wisdom's gates.

The Lord Jesus Christ is the power and wisdom of God. His word will satisfy you, His possessions enrich you, His relationship to God and this world will strike you with awe. He is what you need. If you find Him, you find life. If you don't find Him, you greatly injure yourself. In fact, if you turn away from Him, you love death. This Jesus is the Son of God who came into the world to save sinners. He lived a righteous life, died suffering the wrath of God for His people, and has risen again. He's the one who takes away the sinner's sin—and not because they do right or fix their problems. No, He saves those who trust in Him. Believe in the Lord Jesus, and you will be saved. Find wisdom—that is, find Christ—and you will live.

9

Will You Be Wise or Foolish?

O ne of the really bad ideas among us today is that of neutrality. Many have been duped into thinking they can be a mere spectator. Masses of people believe that when it comes to the big questions of morality, truth, and religion, they can check the box marked "undecided."

But life is not a spectator sport. God has put everyone in the game. The idea of neutrality on these matters is a myth. We cannot say, "Oh, that conversation is not for me. I don't want to fight that battle." By our very existence, we are in the conversation, we are on the battlefield, and bullets are flying.

In other words, it is not *whether* but *which*. It is not whether we will make a decision but which decision we will make. It is not whether we will serve God but which god we will serve. It is not whether we will submit to authority but which authority it will be. It is not whether we will learn lessons but which lessons we will learn.

When it comes to wisdom, we are in a not-whether-but-which situation. Two ladies call out for us. One is lady wisdom, the other lady folly.

It is not whether we will embrace one of these ladies but which lady we will embrace. These ladies are complete opposites. You cannot have them both. You cannot dine with both. You cannot enter both of their homes. Yet, both are pressing their invitations on you. Each person must decide and bear the consequences of his or her decision. Indecision is a decision. Video games have pause buttons, and sporting events include time-outs. But life has no pause button or time-outs. You did not necessarily ask to be on this road with these two ladies crying out to you from the heights. But that's where you are. God has made the world this way. You are at the decision point. Which lady is it going to be?

I have three exhortations for you in this chapter. Each one encourages us to make the good and right decision. The first is decide in favor of lady wisdom. Next, decide to be a wise man, not a scoffer. And finally, decide not in favor of lady folly.

Decide in Favor of Lady Wisdom

We are given a picture of lady wisdom, a picture that gives us many reasons to embrace her (Proverbs 9:1–6).

Right at the outset we see that *she labors.* She's a lady who works. If you embrace this lady, she's going to be a great help to you. Notice all the verbs going on in the first three verses of Proverbs 9. She has *built, hewn, slaughtered, mixed, set, sent.* A flurry of activity is associated with lady wisdom. This lady's work ethic is attractive, a point that can be easily lost on young men today. When looking for a wife, you want to find one who works hard. The marriage relationship is bound up with work. In the beginning, God put Adam in the garden to work it and keep it. It was in that state that it was not good for man to be alone, so God made a helper fit for him. You want a helper who works like lady wisdom. Wisdom is a helpmate who works hard for those who possess her. Get her, and you will be fruitful.

Lady wisdom is not only a hard worker but she works with humility and intelligence. She's humble and smart. We see these qualities in the magnificent house she has constructed—"Wisdom has built her house; she has hewn her seven pillars" (Proverbs 9:1). The seven pillars signal that this is a grand residence. And lady wisdom built it. But, unlike lady folly who is loud, lady wisdom has not said anything while building with such remarkable intelligence. She embodies the call we hear in 1 Thessalonians 4:11 to "aspire to live quietly, and to mind your own affairs, and to work with your hands." Anyone who has seen a strong woman like this working quietly with her hands knows what a beautiful scene this is. If you embrace lady wisdom, you will know how to put in a full day's work without boasting about it to everyone. And you'll reap the benefits of all that quiet work.

We should decide in favor of lady wisdom for she provides a rich banquet. She doesn't provide just any meal; she serves meat. "She has slaughtered her beasts" (Proverbs 9:2). She provides that which satisfies. David says to God in Psalm 63:5–6, "My soul will be satisfied as with fat and rich food . . . when I remember you upon my bed." With lady wisdom, you will get a hearty meal, one that sticks to your ribs and leaves you contented. The enemy has been telling this lie for quite a long time: "The wise way is not the fun way. The wise way is not the pleasurable way." But he has turned the truth upside down. Lady wisdom is serving up a steak dinner.

And she's celebrating while doing so for she has "mixed her wine" (Proverbs 9:2). Wine is associated with joy and gladness in Scripture. Psalm 104:15 says God has given "wine to gladden the heart of man." When God conquers His enemies and brings salvation, He makes a joyful feast of wine. Isaiah 25:6 says, "On this mountain the LORD of hosts will make for all peoples a feast of rich food, a feast of well-aged wine, of rich food full of marrow, of aged wine well refined." It is no surprise, then, to see Christ, who is the wisdom of God, turning water into wine at a wedding feast. He, like lady wisdom mixing her wine, manifests His glory for the joy of His people. If you decide in favor of lady wisdom, you will not only get the good and right way but the happy way.

We should heed the call of lady wisdom for she welcomes the simple. She graciously sends out invitations (Proverbs 9:3). Her welcoming nature is seen in such a generous spreading of the offer. It is not just one but multiple young ladies who are sent out by her. They make their way to the highest places in the town that they might be heard by passersby. Her feast is not a VIP event. You don't have to be part of the in crowd to come to this banquet. We hear her call, "'Whoever is simple, let him turn in here!' To him who lacks sense she says, 'Come, eat of my bread and drink of the wine I have mixed'" (Proverbs 9:4–5). If you lack knowledge, that's okay. You're welcome at this lady's table.

We see a final benefit to deciding in favor of lady wisdom: her guests live (Proverbs 9:6). She calls her guests out of their simple, foolish ways. And in so doing she calls them into something else. She welcomes them to life—life as God intended it to be lived.

What are we to think about lady wisdom and her call? Well, we have in this picture of lady wisdom an opportunity for our affections to be trained. We need to learn what is good. In other words, the reason we don't sit down with wisdom is because we really don't think she's all that great of a lady. The reason we do not meditate on God's Word is because we don't think it satisfies like a steak dinner. The reason we do not commune with Christ is because we don't believe such communion will result in joyful celebration. The reason we don't pray to God for more wisdom is because we don't trust that He is like this gracious lady who has set her table, eager to serve up insight.

So, ask God to show you the beauties of wisdom. Ask Him to help you really believe that the way to experience the good life is to sit down with Christ, in whom are hidden all the treasures of wisdom and knowledge.

Decide to Be a Wise Man, Not a Scoffer

There are not only two ladies to consider but two men as well. We see the wise man and the scoffer (Proverbs 9:7–12). They serve as an interlude between the pictures of the two ladies. We will be one of these men. We're encouraged to decide to be a wise man, not a scoffer. Why? Because the scoffer abuses those who correct him (Proverbs 9:7). Who is the scoffer? Proverbs 21:24 identifies him. There it says that "'scoffer' is the name of the arrogant, haughty man who acts with arrogant pride." This man thinks far too highly of himself. He is incapable of discipline and couldn't find wisdom if it were staring him in the face. You just can't teach this guy anything. The scoffer has an abusive relationship with the truth and those who deliver it to him. That's why Psalm 1 says he's the kind of person we should avoid.

The scoffer not only thunders at his teachers with his hands but he hates them in his heart (Proverbs 9:8). The scoffer hates his reprover because the reprover has touched his god—namely, his own ego. The scoffer worships himself and is ready to declare holy war on those who kick over his idol. What a sad picture. The scoffer rejects the reprover, who is genuinely trying to help. The reprover tells the scoffer, "You don't want to tie yourself to those railroad tracks. There's a truth coming that's not going to change its course because of your opinion." But not only will the scoffer not listen, he burns with anger against this kind truth-teller.

What about the wise man? What does he do when the same truth-teller corrects him? The wise man loves those who correct him (Proverbs 9:8). The wise man doesn't like getting hit by trains. He puts down the ropes, gets off the tracks, and embraces his reprover. Why? The wise man has an entirely different goal than the scoffer. The scoffer seeks his own praise. The wise man seeks the truth. If a reprover helps him to know the truth, then the wise man does not mind the correction; he is grateful for it.

When it comes to reproof, beware of being swept along by the empty-headed ideas abroad today. We live in arrogant days, so we've found all sorts of smoke screens against reproof. Many people are so unsure, individualistic, and sensitive that the whole idea of reproof has flown out the window. Don't require that people be your best friend before they correct you. Don't insist that people experience all that you've experienced before they correct you. Such an attitude smells more like the scoffer than the wise man.

We have another reason to decide to be a wise man. When the wise man is instructed, he becomes even wiser (Proverbs 9:9). When teaching comes to the scoffer, he gets dumber; when it comes to the wise man, he gets wiser. This is the logic of the kingdom of heaven. Jesus says in Matthew 13:12, "For to the one who has, more will be given, and he will have an abundance, but from the one who has not, even what he has will be taken away." If you become a wise man, you will grow in knowledge exponentially.

We see here again how the decision is on us. We *must* decide. There are two roads. The scoffer's road bends sharply and quickly into stupidity. The wise man's road breaks away sharply and quickly into greater wisdom. We should go the way of the wise man for he has the fear of the Lord (Proverbs 9:10). The wise man evidently has this fear of the Lord since it is the beginning of wisdom. Charles Bridges has said, "The fear of the Lord is the affectionate reverence of the child of God by which he bends himself humbly and carefully to his Father's law."[5]

Why is it important to have the fear of the Lord? Because He is worthy to be feared. If you don't fear Him, then that doesn't change this truth about Him. Lacking the fear of God is kind of like entering a cage of hungry lions while saying, "I'm not afraid of hungry lions." Well, who wants to be that guy? Lions don't change their nature based on your feelings. God doesn't either.

So, here we see not only the value of being the wise man, we also see the first step to becoming the wise man: fear the Lord. Acquire this humble reverence that turns you to carefully observe the Father's law. If you are ever going to be the wise man, this is what you need.

This fear of the Lord is important to get because each of these men will reap what they sow. If you plant corn, you will harvest corn, not jellybeans. That's the way God made the world work. Galatians 6:7 says, "Do not be deceived: God is not mocked, for whatever one sows, that will he also reap." That's the principle we see at work with wisdom, for "if you are wise, you are wise to yourself; if you scoff, you alone will bear it" (Proverbs 9:12). If you are wise, your wisdom will serve you. You will have that which yields long life. On the other hand, if you scoff, you will reap the fruit of your scoffing. It will be a heavy burden you will bear alone. An inescapable decision is before every individual, and inescapable consequences attend that decision.

Seeing these two men, we should decide to be the wise man. But to do so we need the fear of the Lord. And to get the fear of the Lord, this affectionate reverence for God, and His Word, we need our hearts to change. Seeing the devastating consequences of being a scoffer and the great blessing of being the wise man should make us yearn for this heart change. But how can we change our affections? We revere certain things. How do we make ourselves revere God? We don't. He does that kind of thing for people. *God saves.* God makes people fear Him and makes those who fear Him fear Him more. We serve the living God. Wisdom comes from Him. Seek Him. Ask Him to give you this fear, this wisdom.

DECIDE NOT IN FAVOR OF LADY FOLLY

We need the fear of God desperately that we might stay away from this nasty lady folly. She really is no good. She can be a tricky lady because it looks at times like she does some of the things lady wisdom does. But when she pretends to be doing the same thing, she's actually doing an entirely different thing. Let's look at this ugly lady so that we might decide not in favor of her.

To begin, we see that she is a lazy thief. How different she is than the hard-working lady wisdom. There are no verbs showing the flurry of activity we saw with lady wisdom. What is lady folly doing? "She *sits* at the door of her house" (Proverbs 9:14). Even when she goes up to the high places, she sits herself down. This sluggardly woman has not produced anything for her guests to eat. She has stolen the water she offers to her guests (Proverbs 9:17). The fool and the sluggard are close companions in the book of Proverbs. Proverbs 26:13 speaks of the lazy fool. It says, "The sluggard says, 'There is a lion in the road! There is a lion in the streets!'" Like this lazy lady, the fool fabricates reasons for not getting to work.

We should reject this lady's call since, in addition to her lazy, thieving ways, she is boisterously ignorant. She's the opposite of lady wisdom, who silently built her house. Where are lady folly's seven pillars? They are nonexistent. But she does have something that lady wisdom lacked: a whole lot of talk. Lady folly "is loud; she is seductive and knows nothing" (Proverbs 9:13). This is really a bad combination. It is one thing to talk too much but quite another to be ignorant. To be an ignorant talker is double-plus no good. This lady invites you to her house, but she has all the ingredients of the quarrelsome wife. Proverbs 21:9 says "it is better to live in a corner of the housetop" than with her.

We should turn a deaf ear to this lady's call for she provides only water and bread (Proverbs 9:17). This foolish woman has not slaughtered any beasts. She does not have fat and rich food. The foolish life really is lame. Proverbs 13:15 says, "The way of the transgressor is hard"(ASV). But the foolish sinner will not admit his way is hard. If it were not so sad it would be comical to watch him pretend that his way is easy, that his stolen water is "sweet." Fools give great attention to presenting their bread and water as if it were something more than bread and water. The book of Judges gives us a good picture of what happens when everyone acts foolish. What's the fruit? War, assassination, people's eyes getting plucked out, a woman being horribly abused then chopped up into many pieces. Look at this lady's food. And pretend not that folly is fruitful.

We have another reason to tell this woman to quiet down up there on the heights. She eats in secret, alone (Proverbs 9:17). Lady wisdom prepared a table where wine and true companions abounded. Lady folly seems to lock her guests up in a solitary dungeon and pretend that it is a pleasurable experience. The fool will find himself increasingly alone. Like the scoffer who has hated and abused all those who sought to correct him, the fool is left without any friends.

We should decline lady folly's offer for she targets the simple. After taking her seat on the highest places of the town, she's "calling to those who pass by, who are going straight on their way, [saying,] 'Whoever is simple, let him turn in here!" (Proverbs 9:15). She speaks to those who lack sense. Well, here this lady's deception appears. She's doing something very much like lady wisdom. But where lady wisdom was graciously welcoming even the simple and undeserving, lady folly is targeting the susceptible, senseless passersby. Here is the lesson for us. Beware of foolishness. Foolishness is not merely something you may fall into along the way. It is something that comes after you. You don't have to go out looking for foolishness. It will come looking for you. All you need to do to become a fool is nothing.

A final reason to avoid this woman like the plague is that her guests are dead. The fool has been played, for "he does not know that the dead are there, that her guests are in the depths of Sheol" (Proverbs 9:18). We have seen this about lady folly before. She is not only a killer, but a stealthy killer. Notice, "*he does not know* that the dead are there." The guy who has heeded her call from the heights is blindly headed into a death trap. Lady folly won't only serve you a lame meal. Yes, she will do that. Your life will lack color and vitality if you decide in her favor. But after your lackluster life, there will come a bitter end. She not only wants to drain away your life, she wants to snuff it out completely—and she will, so don't accept her invitation.

There are two ways before us. Awaken from the pipe dream of neutrality. The decision is upon us. Lady wisdom and lady folly both call to you. Which lady is it going to be?

Christians need to have the mind of Christ in a day that's set on ignoring Him. We need to relish His ways in a time when people are doing their best to disregard them. We must speak honestly about the goodness of God's wisdom and the insanity of anything else.

And we need not only speak about the wisdom of His ways but demonstrate it by living wisely. Sit down at lady wisdom's house, eat, drink, and celebrate. Show the world how rich and fat God's ways are. Illustrate to the world all the good things that happen when you affectionately revere God and His ways. Diligently pursue Christ, who is wisdom, and grow wiser and wiser like the wise man. Be set apart from the scoffing world so that the distinction grows ever wider. In so doing, you love your neighbor, for they will see how pleasant a life of wisdom and godliness is.

Surely as you look at these two ladies and two men, you can see the goodness of the one and the outright silliness of the other. Remember that the world will not wait on you to make a decision. In the Old Testament, a man named Joshua stood before the Israelites. He was crossing over the Jordan River to conquer God's enemies. He said to Israel, "Choose this day whom you will serve. . . . As for me and my house, we will serve the Lord" (Joshua 24:15). The same call is before you today. It is not whether you will bow to a lord but which lord will it be. It is not whether you will trust someone but which person you will trust. It is not whether you will receive one of these ladies' invitations but which invitation you will receive.

The way to embrace wisdom is to embrace Jesus Christ. He is the Son of God, who became a man to live, die, and rise again for sinners like you and me. He suffered for foolish people like you and me. He suffered the loud screams of fools. He endured the ignorant blows of Roman soldiers. He was hated and abused by scoffers. He walked a lonely road often having to eat His bread in secret. He suffered God's judgment so that His people wouldn't. He suffered the bitter fruit of foolishness so that simple people like us might be welcomed into the wedding feast.

But when He calls you to come, you must come. If you go off to care for worldly affairs, He will fill up the wedding hall so there will be no more room. And you must have a wedding garment, the wedding garment of righteousness. Only those with perfection can attend this wedding celebration. You and I don't have that righteousness. But Jesus Christ does, and His righteousness is yours through faith. Trust Him, turning from your sins, and you will sit down at His table for an eternal celebration.

10

WISDOM: WHERE TO FIND IT

One of the reasons people don't get wisdom is because they don't want it. They do not find it appealing. The book of Proverbs has much to tell us on this front. It motivates us to get wisdom. Get wisdom, the Proverbs say, because it is better than gold.

But there is another reason people don't get wisdom: they don't know where to find it. They may have determined it is good to get but simply don't know where to start. And who could blame them? We have numerous voices coming at us. We live in a world with people, movies, books, teachings, podcasts, social media, and the like. Notifications come at us from every side. People shape us more than we want to admit. And we get shaped quickly into believing that certain people "have it together."

We look up to people. We have role models. Sadly, many people get into all sorts of trouble because they have bad ones. They think they are with the right folks, but alas, they are not with the right ones. We can't escape paying the consequences for hanging around with the wrong people. But there is an upside. We will reap the benefits of good company—"Whoever walks with the wise becomes wise, but the companion of fools will suffer harm" (Proverbs 13:20).

Wisdom, then, is found among the wise. If you hang out with the wise, you will likely become wise. If you hang around with fools, you will likely become like them. I want to consider three questions in this chapter: (1) Does everyone have wisdom, (2) what do the wise possess, and (3) what do the wise do?

DOES EVERYONE HAVE WISDOM?

It is self-evident that everyone does not possess wisdom. You do not have to live long to discover this truth. The wise possess wisdom, and fools do not. These two are not at peace. The wise and the foolish are locked in an inevitable battle. We find ourselves on this battlefield. Neutrality is not an option. Pretending like the battle does not exist is a fool's errand, which leaves you still on the side of the losing team, just masquerading like you are not.

For example, the "coexist" bumper sticker is one of the most nonsensical things you could put on the back of your car. It portrays many different world religions and ideologies, with a summons for everyone to get along. But these religions and ideologies have radically different understandings of love, law, justice, salvation, joy, courage, and many other central pillars of life. The coexist idea says, "All your deep convictions are really not that different; there is a bit of wisdom found in all these faiths." But that is not what Scripture teaches us.

God says that the fool has no wisdom but the wise man has plenty of it. Proverbs 14:7 instructs, "Leave the presence of a fool, for there you do not meet words of knowledge." You may find a lot of things in the presence of a fool, but you won't find wisdom because "the fool says in his heart, 'There is no God'" (Psalm 14:1). "Fools despise wisdom and instruction" (Proverbs 1:7). They do so because "the way of the fool is right in his own eyes" (Proverbs 12:15). The fool's dilemma is not merely that he lacks knowledge. He also lacks good—"For my people are foolish; they know me not; they are stupid children; they have no understanding. They are 'wise'—in doing evil! But how to do good they know not" (Jeremiah 4:22).

The fool cannot find wisdom if he tries, but the wise man can. Proverbs 14:6 says, "A scoffer seeks wisdom in vain, but knowledge is easy for a man of understanding." It is bad enough that wisdom is no companion to the fool. But the trouble mounts when you see that a fool can't track wisdom down. Such a man is void of the necessary ingredients. He has no awareness of God. He does not have the Spirit. He is bankrupt when it comes to knowledge of the Word of God. How different is the man of understanding. He knows the living God. He is inhabited by the Spirit and thus can understand the things freely revealed by the Almighty.

It follows that the fool has more folly coming, and the wise man more knowledge coming. The fool cannot find wisdom, but folly can find him. Proverbs 14:18 says, "The simple inherit folly, but the prudent are crowned with knowledge." Folly is attracted to the fool. Foolishness comes to the fool like a family heirloom. We often do not know what we will inherit, much less what others will. But when you are talking to a fool, you know what he is going to receive as an inheritance.

This is the logic of the kingdom. Jesus says, "For to the one who has, more will be given, and he will have an abundance, but from the one who has not, even what he has will be taken away" (Matthew 13:12). Wisdom begets wisdom, and folly begets folly. That is one reason we should be quick about getting wisdom at the outset—"God is not mocked, for whatever ones sows, that will he also reap" (Galatians 6:7).

Not only does the fool get more folly but he shares it. He promotes folly, while the wise man promotes wisdom. Proverbs 13:16 says, "Every prudent man acts with knowledge, but a fool flaunts his folly." The fool cannot help but have his foolishness displayed. Neither can the wise man suppress his wisdom. Both trees will bear fruit. People will take a bite of each. The fool flaunts his folly in his relationship with God. He claims there is no God and teaches others the same. He acts as if sin is fruitful, family is insignificant, and work is meaningless.

Nevertheless, there is hope, for the prudent man acts too, and he does so with knowledge. You can watch a wise man and see knowledge at work. You observe the wise man cultivate a relationship with God in awe and joy. He hates sin and labors to put it to death. He leads his family, entrusting them to God. He labors, knowing that God has called him to work and exercise dominion.

Folly and wisdom cannot be kept secret, for the fool speaks folly but the wise man speaks knowledge. Proverbs 15:2 says, "The tongue of the wise commends knowledge, but the mouths of fools pour out folly." Likewise, Proverbs 15:7 says, "The lips of the wise spread knowledge; not so the hearts of fools." And oh, how much talking there is today! We have greater access to the wise and the foolish than ever before. We really should take notice. We are going one way or the other, and in a hurry.

How do fools speak folly? The ways are more than can be counted. But here are a few. The fool will speak peace when there is no peace. He is really good at calming people down when they need to go to war. The fool will speak harsh words when soft ones are necessary. He is known for yelling at the wrong time. He forgets that "with patience a ruler may be persuaded, and a soft tongue will break a bone" (Proverbs 25:15). The fool will speak lies about God directly, then he cannot help muddying up everything downstream, like love, happiness, courage, beauty, and more. The fool will speak both flattery and slander. He does not mind saying things that are false in both directions.

The wise man is just the opposite. He speaks sound words. How does the wise man speak wisdom? He speaks fitting words. He knows when to speak and when not to. For "a word fitly spoken is like apples of gold in a setting of silver" (Proverbs 25:11). He speaks these fitting words when correction is called for. Rather than the fool's flattery, the wise man will speak honestly and lovingly. He has a knack for speaking words of true comfort. He knows what promise fits the predicament a particular friend is in. Ultimately, the wise speak truth about God and, therefore, all that is downstream, including love, happiness, courage, beauty, and much more.

The wise and the foolish have different relationships with the wicked. The fool praises the wicked, but the wise man fights against them. Proverbs 28:4 says, "Those who forsake the law praise the wicked, but those who keep the law strive against them." Well-meaning people make a common error. That is, they make peace with the wicked. Far too many people just cannot stomach the fight against wickedness. So, they make some kind of truce. But such people are not wise. The wise offer themselves freely in the day of Christ's power as He drives back wickedness (Psalm 110:3).

The world declares, "Be true to yourself," and "To each their own." They cry, "Don't be judgey. Who are you to be telling others how to live?" They say, "All roads lead to God, and good, take the one that best suits you." But God says, "The wise have wisdom and fools do not."

What Do the Wise Possess?

Having seen that everyone does not have wisdom, I turn to the question, What do the wise possess? The question is significant, for most people will agree that not everyone is wise. The natural question one will ask, then, is, "Where can I find the wise people?" One way you can identify them is by what they possess.

Wise people possess the fear of the Lord. Proverbs 15:33 says, "The fear of the Lord is instruction in wisdom, and humility comes before honor." This is the central possession, the foundational possession. All the other possessions grow out of this one. If this one is missing, the others cannot be present. For "the fear of the LORD is the *beginning* of wisdom, and the knowledge of the Holy One is insight" (Proverbs 9:10). And how could it be otherwise, seeing "no wisdom, no understanding, no counsel can avail against the LORD" (Proverbs 21:30)?

The fear of the Lord is the healthy reverence that God's children have for their Father, who is their creator, redeemer, and judge. The fear of the Lord moves God's children to humbly trust and obey Him. If you don't have this fear of the Lord, you will never be able to live wisely in His world. Proverbs 3:19 says, "The LORD by wisdom founded the earth; by understanding he established the heavens."

If you want to get the fear of the Lord, then you must receive it from the Lord. You cannot increase this fear in yourself one ounce apart from the Spirit's work. When the Spirit gives someone this fear, that person will possess wisdom and, in turn, will possess a healthy understanding of authority. They will know how appropriately to both exercise authority and submit to authority. The wise father exhorts his son, saying, "Hear, my son, your father's instruction, and forsake not your mother's teaching" (Proverbs 1:8). The authority of both father and mother is in view—"My son, keep your father's commandment, and forsake not your mother's teaching" (Proverbs 6:20). The wise father and mother understand their God-given authority and, thus, their God-given responsibility. They are not permitted to parent willy-nilly. Fathers are to raise their children "in the discipline and instruction of the Lord" (Ephesians 6:4).

Likewise, the wise man knows what it means to be under authority. He knows how to honor and submit to those God has established in positions of authority, be they civil, ecclesiastical, or familial. Our times are steeped in foolish egalitarian thought. The wise understand that God has established a hierarchical world both in the heavens and on the earth. So, they look to the King of Kings in order to live well in that divinely ordered world.

The wise also possess a love for discipline. Proverbs 12:1 says, "Whoever loves discipline loves knowledge, but he who hates reproof is stupid." There is, of course, discomfort with discipline. We are not to like reproof for the sake of reproof. But we are to love discipline because it propels us to greater knowledge. The disciplined man has a hold on his appetites while the undisciplined man's appetites have a hold on him.

Along with discipline, the wise possess patience. Proverbs 17:27 says, "He who has a cool spirit is a man of understanding." Likewise, "Whoever is slow to anger has great understanding, but he who has a hasty temper exalts folly" (Proverbs 14:29). The text does not say the man of understanding never gets angry. Many a man has pretended to be wise by being an easy-going guy who never gets his feathers ruffled. In many cases, such a man simply does not care about what God cares about. He does not hate what is evil. He does not love what is good. Even so, the wise man is slow to anger. He does not have a hot temper. The man who is easily angered has a problem with God. At the bottom, such a man does not like the way God is ruling His universe. That guy is not a fountain of wisdom and knowledge.

The wise also possess humility, for "with the humble is wisdom" (Proverbs 11:2). Humility does not mean that an individual thinks very low of himself—"I'm not much, but I'm all I ever think about!" Humility, rather, is a fruit of the fear of the Lord. The humble man thinks about himself with accurate judgment. He knows he is not God. He knows there is not a single thing he has that he did not receive (1 Corinthians 4:7).

Joy in understanding will be found among the wise. It is not so with the fool, for he "takes no pleasure in understanding, but only in expressing his opinion" (Proverbs 18:2). If you find yourself talking too much, one of the things that can really help is obtaining a renewed desire to understand. Understanding requires not only speaking but listening to others. We will be more eager to do so when we really want to learn. What a world there is to explore. Christians can learn about God, their creator and redeemer. We can learn at least some of the innumerable blessings bound up in our salvation. We take joy in knowing the truth about God. We can observe how the world works—how trees, squirrels, businesses, economics, governments, homes, and robots work. "The earth is the LORD's and the fullness thereof" (Psalm 24:1). Since we are His, and we are given His Spirit and His Word, what a wealth of knowledge there is for us to understand. The wise man says, "I'm far too busy learning to be about endlessly expressing my opinion."

WHAT DO THE WISE DO?

We have discovered some ways to identify the wise, considering how important it is to do so. Along with marking what the wise possess, we can also take notice of what they do.

For starters, the wise hear the law. The wise father warns, "Cease to hear instruction, my son, and you will stray from the words of knowledge"

(Proverbs 19:27). Similarly, "If one turns away his ear from hearing the law, even his prayer is an abomination" (Proverbs 28:9). The law of the Lord is good. By meditating on it and delighting in it day and night, we will be like that tree planted by streams of water bearing fruit in season (Psalm 1). The bedrock reason the wise love God's law is because they love God. It is, after all, His law. How could we not hear it and rejoice in it?

The wise not only hear but obey the law. Proverbs 29:18 says, "Where there is no prophetic vision the people cast off restraint, but blessed is he who keeps the law." The law-keeper is "a son with understanding" (Proverbs 28:7). James says we must not be mere hearers of the Word but doers of the Word as well. What a dreadful thing to routinely listen to God's Word only to go and live contrary to it. And on the upside, what a rich life it is to hear God's Word and believe and obey it. We will certainly not obey perfectly, but we will be able to point to a pattern of obedience as we trust in God.

In addition to hearing and obeying God's law, the wise seek knowledge. Proverbs 15:14 says, "The heart of him who has understanding seeks knowledge, but the mouths of fools feed on folly." One of the truly lamentable things about our present age is what an abundance of folly is served up like an all-you-can-eat buffet. We scroll through Facebook, flick through Twitter, and feast on folly nightly on Amazon, Netflix, or YouTube. All these media channels can be used for the pursuit of knowledge, of course. But that does not mean that most people do so. The wise, on the other hand, do not consider themselves too good for more knowledge. They know God is infinitely glorious, and therefore, they will never discover all there is to know about Him or His creation.

The wise not only seek out but they also restrain—they restrain words. Proverbs 17:27 says, "Whoever restrains his words has knowledge." Likewise, "Whoever belittles his neighbor lacks sense, but a man of understanding remains silent" (Proverbs 11:12). The wise restrain untrue words. Lies are told at many times and in many places, but the wise man holds back from lies. He also restrains unfitting words. Perhaps a word is true, but it need not be said at the time. He restrains from speaking too many words. Even when words are fitting, wisdom knows when to stop. Then the wise restrain words in the presence of fools. They know how not to cast their pearls before swine (Matthew 7:6).

The wise know when it is time to move on. They move on when others delight in sinful pleasures. Proverbs 15:21 says, "Folly is a joy to him who lacks sense, but a man of understanding walks straight ahead." The wise are not stagnant. They are not lazy or lost. They know they have a place to be going and they know how to get to that place. The wise are not easily knocked off course for they have prepared for temptations, use God's Word as a lamp to their feet, and have their sights set to joy in Christ.

It not, however, as if the wise know everything. And better yet, they don't think they do. So they take advice, seeing that "by insolence comes nothing but strife, but with those who take advice is wisdom" (Proverbs 13:10). There is a type of man who claims he loves the truth, but he will not hear it from anyone else. He claims he loves the Bible, but he will only pay attention to it if his own eyes are reading the words. He does not like taking counsel from others. Such a man is not wise. There is a similar character. He seeks advice from everyone around. In fact, you cannot find a person whom he has not asked for counsel on any particular in his life. But in all his asking for advice, he still has this problem: he does not take it. He does not actually do what is prescribed but finds some other route that is more comfortable or suitable to him. Such a man is not wise. The wise *take advice*.

More than that, the wise receive reproof. Proverbs 29:15 teaches, "The rod and reproof give wisdom, but a child left to himself brings shame to his mother." Wise people do not only welcome you when you counsel them but also when you correct them. Surely it is easier to receive a word of encouragement rather than the rod of correction. But they are both truth. The only difference between the two is *us*. In the first scenario we are already in step with the truth. In the latter, we are out of step with it. Why would we love the truth in one situation and not the other? The truth is the same. There is a word to parents here. Seeing what a wonderful thing it is to be wise, we should be faithful to bring the rod and reproof to our children. If we don't, we leave our children to be a shame to their mothers.

Wisdom is found among the wise. This being the case, we should seek out the wisest men and women if we would grow in wisdom. But the wisest man you will ever find is the Lord Jesus Christ. He is the one who has done battle against the foolish Serpent. He is the one crowned with knowledge. He is the one who has laid up wisdom. He is the one who has all the glorious possessions we have considered. He has the fear of the Lord and all that comes with it. He is the long-suffering servant. He has humility. He has heard and obeyed the law. He restrained His words, for He opened not His mouth. He moved right ahead toward the cross, setting His face toward Jerusalem while others went after worldly pleasures and Satan's devices. If you would find wisdom, then find Christ. In Him are hidden all the treasures of wisdom and knowledge. He is the Son of God and the Son of Man. Trust in Him, and you will be wise.

11

THE SCALES BELONG TO THE LORD

O ne of the problems we see in the world is that people want justice but they do not want God. Yet you can't have one without the other. God and justice fly tandem. So those who pursue justice apart from God end up pursuing injustice. Those who demand justice while ignoring God end up perverting justice.

Such people do not have the *pursuing justice* part wrong; they have the *ignoring God* part wrong. The pursuing justice part is glorious. "And what does the LORD require of you but to do justice, and to love kindness, and to walk humbly with your God?" (Micah 6:8). But there *He* is again. If you do not walk humbly with God, then you are not going to do justice.

In this chapter I want to demonstrate why this is true, why you can't do justice without God.

Proverbs 16:11 says, "A just balance and scales are the LORD's; all the weights in the bag are his work." The scales of justice belong to the Lord. That is why you cannot do justice without Him. He possesses the standard of justice. He is the measuring rod. He is the *definition* of righteousness and justice. God's law is the official yardstick. We live in a society that has rejected God's yardstick and begun making their own. They measure them out to a size of their own liking. No matter that they are two feet or one foot or four feet—"To each their own," they say. But then they begin measuring stuff with them. You see the problem? "You sold me a yard of fabric, but according to *my yardstick*, it is not a yard!" If you want justice, then you must know the standard. And the standard is the Lord's. The scales of justice belong to Him.

There can be a lot of confusion these days about who is just and who is not. So we will take three main teachings from Proverbs. First, God is just; second, the righteous are just; third, the wise are just.

God Is Infinitely Just

First, if we're going to think rightly about justice, then we must not only consider the scales of justice but the one holding the scales. That is God. He is *infinitely* just.

God not only does what is just but, first and foremost, He *is* just. Deuteronomy 32:4 says, "The Rock, . . . a God of faithfulness and without iniquity, just and upright is he." In this regard God is entirely different than mankind. We can find people who are more upright than others. But we cannot find people who are *perfectly* upright. We cannot find people without iniquity. Romans 3:23 says, "For all have sinned and fall short of the glory of God." We have fallen short of God's righteousness, but God has not fallen short of it. He is exactly as He ought to be because He is God. He does not wake up every morning trying to keep His standards. Earthly fathers do this. Our heavenly Father does not. He does not have to *try to keep* the standard of righteousness; He *is* the standard of righteousness. This truth has huge implications for creatures created in His image.

Being infinitely just, God abominates injustice. Proverbs 11:1 says, "A false balance is an abomination to the LORD." It is the unjust man who uses a false balance. He carries a stone marked five pounds that is actually six pounds so that when it's placed in the scales, he skims an extra pound from his customers. God is very displeased with such a man. But be careful to understand—God is not only displeased with ancient Israelite merchants who carried false weights. The proverb teaches that God abominates any and all unjust men, men who do not do what is right and true.

The upside is God delights in the just. Proverbs 11:1 continues, "A just weight is his delight." God is happy with the man who carries a five-pound stone that is marked five pounds, a man who does what is right and true. But God does not simply delight in an accurately labeled stone. God does not delight in the man who carries a just weight on Tuesday and a false weight on Wednesday. He does not delight in a man who carries a just weight in his left pocket and a false weight in his right. The proverb teaches that God delights in the man who is truly just, entirely just.

But how do we know who the just man is? We must remember that "a just balance and scales are the LORD's" (Proverbs 16:11). God is the one who determines who is just and unjust. He has a standard by which He judges the world. The scales of justice, the scales God possesses, have been revealed to us in His law. His law is the perfect standard by which we will be judged. If we would be just, then we must measure up to the very righteousness of God revealed to us in the Ten Commandments.

It is at this point that some might try to escape God's just ways. Measuring ourselves against the Ten Commandments doesn't look so good for any of us. So, some people mistakenly believe that God will declare them to be just if they simply offer Him a bit of sacrifice. They may not have perfectly obeyed the Ten Commandments ("Who has?" they think), but they've done right by God by giving Him some money in the plate every now and then, by attending a decent amount of religious services, perhaps even offering some perfunctory prayers at meal times. But Proverbs 21:3 says, "To do righteousness and justice is more acceptable to the LORD than sacrifice." When Israel offered up their sacrifices with unjust hands, God replied, "Even though you offer me your burnt offerings and grain offerings, I will not accept them; and the peace offerings of your fattened animals, I will not look upon them. Take away from me the noise of your songs; to the melody of your harps I will not listen. But let *justice* roll down like waters, and *righteousness* like an ever-flowing stream" (Amos 5:22–24). Thus, God delights in those who live uprightly, in perfect conformity to His law, and there is no shortcut through sacrificial gifts.

God's delight in justice, which seems so right in one sense, has now in another sense become quite uncomfortable for us who have not perfectly obeyed the Ten Commandments. And if anyone is counting, that is *all of us*. We might prefer the proverb to teach that "God delights in our best efforts no matter how far short we come up." Or "God delights in our good intentions and some religious rituals to make up for the shortfall." But God's Word to us is "If you would be just, then you must be perfect like Me, the just God."

Since we cannot escape by only meeting some of God's standards plus a little sacrifice, we human beings are known for another attempt to escape God's justice. We simply throw off God's standard, construct our own, and justify people accordingly. But what really happens here is that we start justifying those who are not really just. That is, we start justifying the wicked. And Proverbs 17:15 says, "He who justifies the wicked . . . [is] an abomination to the LORD." We do ourselves great harm when we make up our own standards and proceed to declare ourselves just. If we were in charge of the scales, then we would be fine. But we are most certainly not in charge of the scales, so we are merely kidding ourselves with our little two-foot-long yardsticks. And in the meantime, we are storing up God's anger against us.

There is no escape through meeting some of God's standards plus sacrifice. There is no escape through creating our own standards and justifying ourselves. But there is an escape from the judgment of God. His name is Jesus Christ, the righteous. He is the one who measures up to the Ten Commandments. He has lived, died, and risen again so that His people might have His righteousness as their very own. Those who trust in Christ receive His perfection and are declared to be just by the infinitely just God.

Here is great hope. God has seen fit to give His very own righteousness to those who, not measuring up to His perfect scales, trust in Jesus His Son, depend on Him, call on Him. Those who do that are saved from God's coming judgment.

THE RIGHTEOUS ARE CATEGORICALLY JUST

Upon being saved we become the righteous, categorically so. Those in Christ are righteous, and those not in Christ are unrighteous. Now, we Christians are not just in the same way God is. God is infinitely just in Himself. We are scoundrels in ourselves but righteous and just in Christ. A number of proverbs teach us that those who are righteous in Christ have a harmonious relationship with justice, while those who are not righteous in Christ have a contentious relationship with justice.

We see, for example, that the righteous understand justice. Proverbs 28:5 says, "Evil men do not understand justice, but those who seek the LORD understand it completely." The problem is not only that evil men fail do justice; the problem is they fail to understand it. They don't know where to begin. If presented with a situation calling for justice, they lack what is necessary to render an accurate verdict. Many walk around America today crying, "We want justice. When do we want it? Now!" And they simply do not know what they are asking for. Remember, just scales belong to the Lord. If this is so, then you must understand the Lord if you're going to understand just scales. Who knows the Lord? Not the evil but the righteous. Those who seek God, the proverb says.

The righteous not only understand justice, they respect it. Proverbs 19:28 states, "A worthless witness mocks at justice, and the mouth of the wicked devours iniquity." The wicked cannot help but ridicule justice. They ridicule justice because they ridicule the law. They ridicule the law because they ridicule the Lawgiver, whose name is God. This is what occurs in Psalm 2 where "the kings of the earth set themselves, and the rulers take counsel together, against the LORD and against His Anointed, saying, 'Let us burst their bonds apart and cast away their cords from us.'" The problem with them doing so is that God mocks back. He laughs at their laughing and goes forth with His justice despite their disdain for Him. The righteous, on the other hand, revere the One holding the scales of justice and therefore respect His scales.

This being the case, the righteous provide just counsel. Proverbs 12:5 says, "The thoughts of the righteous are just; the counsels of the wicked are deceitful." How can you give just advice if you don't understand justice and laugh at it? But the righteous have the mind of Christ, therefore, they can understand things of God. Therefore, they are in position to provide counsel without deceit. Young people should mark this well. You will find all sorts of people happy to provide you counsel. Much of it will be lousy. How do you know to whom you should listen? Listen to the counsel of the just. Listen to the counsel of the righteous. Take your cues from those who are in Christ and like Christ. If you take counsel from the unjust, you will find yourself at odds with God's scales of justice.

The relationship between the righteous and justice continues as we see the righteous rejoice when justice is done. Proverbs 21:15 says, "When justice is done, it is a joy to the righteous but terror to evildoers." In this fallen world, justice is not always done. Things are not entirely as they ought to be. Yet at times, justice is done. Verdicts are rendered that accord with the scales that belong to the Lord. When this kind of thing happens, the wicked are scared out of their socks. They are outlaws down here. When God's law is enforced, they find themselves on the wrong end of justice. But the righteous have nothing to fear. Rather they rejoice! When justice is done, they are getting what they pray for. Jesus taught us to pray, "Your kingdom come, your will be done, on earth as it is in heaven" (Matthew 6:10). When God's will is done on earth, then justice is done on earth. We are not speaking merely about justice in the sense of God rendering out punishment on the wicked. That is a part of it. But when justice is done, we also see the reward of the righteous. They "get justice," which is a good thing. We rejoice when justice is done because God's ways are becoming our ways.

Since the righteous long for this kind of thing, they refuse to cheat justice. Proverbs 17:23 says, "The wicked accepts a bribe in secret to pervert the ways of justice." The wicked are happy to take what they can at the expense of justice. That is what they're doing with that six-pound stone marked five pounds. They are in it for their own pockets, not the kingdom of God. The righteous, however, live for Christ. They rejoice at His ways being established on earth and therefore do not take a bribe. The temptation to cheat is a strong one, especially when no one is looking. "Cheaters never prosper" is a good old saying that can help. But we have here a stronger truth that can aid us when we want to cheat. When we do so, *we are perverting God's scales*. Remember, the scales belong to Him. "Why are you leaning on my scales?" God asks. He sees you tinkering with His stuff. So the righteous refuse to cheat justice.

As a result, the righteous know the peace that accords with justice. Proverbs 21:7 says, "The violence of the wicked will sweep them away, because they refuse to do what is just." Now we are getting down to some of the sweetest truth. What happens to the wicked when they refuse to do what is just? They get swept away, scattered by the wind. The way of the transgressor is hard. The sorrows of those who go after other gods shall multiply (Psalm 16:4). You don't break God's law, you break yourself against God's law, as the saying goes. Cheaters never win in the end. Doing injustice is not only wrong, it is stupid. If you drink poison, you're just not going to have a good day. This is a natural law that does not budge. Likewise, if you do injustice, life will not be a sunny day at the beach. Why? The scales of justice belong to the Lord. If it were someone else holding the scales, you might be able to change things, but this is the Lord we are talking about. He will ensure that we reap what we sow. This being so, the righteous enjoy the peaceful fruit of just living. They are in harmony with the way God has designed the world, not drinking poison and obeying God's law.

Finally, because the righteous are categorically just, they abominate the unjust. Proverbs 29:27 says, "An unjust man is an abomination to the righteous, but one whose way is straight is an abomination to the wicked." No peace subsists between these two peoples. How could there be? What fellowship does light have with darkness? The righteous shine like stars amid a crooked and twisted generation. The righteous know God, understand justice, speak just words, delight when justice is done, refuse to cheat, and reap the peaceful fruit of just living. While, on the other side of things, the wicked do not know God, thus they know not justice, speak crooked things, fear justice being done, cut corners, and are swept away through injustice.

What are we to do in light of these things? When you hear talk of justice, remember the categories of the righteous in Christ and the wicked outside of Christ. Many today are losing sight of these categories for other categories. They speak of divisions between the haves and have-nots, old and young, men and women, light-skinned and dark-skinned, heterosexual and homosexual. Then with these divisions they take man-made scales and cry out for justice.

What are we to do? By all means, we should render to all people what they are due. In other words, we are to live justly. And we should happily render people in these various categories what they are due. But we will not be able to do so if we lose sight of these two truths: (1) the righteous are just, and (2) the scales belong to the Lord. If you would know what a man is due, look to the One holding the scales of justice. Look to His law.

THE WISE ARE PRACTICALLY JUST

If we are going to live this way, then we need what Proverbs calls wisdom. We need to know God's truth and what to do with it. We must have *knowledge* to live in accordance with the scales of justice—we must be practically just. If we would live justly, then we must get wisdom. And if we would get wisdom, then we need to work hard and know what needs to be done.

It takes hard work to get wisdom. The wise father says to his son, "My son, if you receive my words and treasure up my commandments with you, making your ear attentive to wisdom and inclining your heart to understanding; yes, if you call out for insight and raise your voice for understanding, if you seek it like silver and search for it as for hidden treasures, · · · then you will understand righteousness and justice and equity" (Proverbs 2:1–4, 9).

We should not mistake being categorically just with being practically just. Some Christians can make really foolish decisions, truly bad judgments. To avoid this and do justice in the world we must seek after wisdom like a hidden treasure. Listen to those imperatives: receive my words, treasure up my commandments, make your ear attentive, incline your heart, call out, search for. If you don't get after wisdom, and seriously so, then you will fail to live justly in the world.

What needs to be done? Gather with God's people to hear God's truth. Meditate on the Word of God personally. Give yourself to study. Devote yourself as a family to God's truth. Seek out a wise Christian to spend time with. Ask God that your heart be inclined to wisdom.

The chief thing that must be done to get wisdom is to get Christ. In Proverbs 8, wisdom is personified. Wisdom says in that chapter, verse 8, "All the words of my mouth are righteous; there is nothing twisted or crooked in them." Again, in verse 20 of that chapter, "*I* walk in the way of righteousness, in the paths of justice." Who is this wisdom who walks in the paths of justice who speaks straight words? It is Christ. In Christ are found all the treasures of wisdom and knowledge. You cannot get wisdom without getting Christ. He is where you must go to find it.

We live in very unjust times, and yet people are zealous for so-called justice. You can see what is going on. They have neglected the true standard and are very committed to measuring yards by their two-foot-long homemade sticks. We have no reason to fear, but there is good reason to let out a hearty belly laugh. God does. Why? Because the scales of justice belong to the Lord, all the weights in the bag are His work.

12

BUILDING AND FIGHTING IN THE DAY OF ADVERSITY

Every person builds and fights. There are no exceptions. Some are building healthy households. Others are building temples of destruction. Some are fighting the fight of faith, and others are fighting against the faithful. Some are doing battle well, while some, poorly. Some are building their homes on the rock. Others are building on shifting sand. But every person builds and fights in one direction or the other.

It is also true that we are all building and fighting under pressure. We lay bricks and unsheathe swords beneath a hot, scorching sun, a sun that has a way of firming up those who belong to God and melting away those who do not. No one is exempt from the heat.

This being the case, God's people must get wisdom to build and fight well in the day of adversity. You need wisdom if you're going to build and fight. You especially need it in the day of adversity—"If you faint in the day of adversity, your strength is small" (Proverbs 24:10). The sweltering heat of such difficult days will come upon every one of us. What do you need? Wisdom. Life in the world God made is high stakes: build or die; fight well or suffer defeat. Get wisdom, or you will fail in the day of adversity.

Consider the fool and what he's building, then the wise man and what he is building. Finally, we will consider the heat of the day of adversity.

THE FOOLISH MAN BUILDS A HOUSE OF DESTRUCTION

We can learn a lot by negation. To better grasp what something is, you can make a start by knowing what it is not. The wise man is not the fool. He doesn't build like the fool builds. We should know the fool and his methods.

Who is the fool? The fool is the one who says in his heart, "There is no God" (Psalm 14:1). He despises wisdom and instruction (Proverbs 1:7). His ways are right in his own eyes (Proverbs 12:15). God tells us through the prophet Jeremiah, "For my people are foolish; they know me not; they are stupid children; they have no understanding. They are 'wise'—in doing evil! But how to do good they know not" (Jeremiah 4:22).

The foolish man's heart studies destruction (Proverbs 24:2). He knows how to ruin a good thing. Lady folly tears her house down with her own hands (Proverbs 14:1). The righteous destroy things too. The apostle Paul says the righteous have weapons to tear down strongholds (2 Corinthians 10:4). But the righteous destroy the strongholds of God's enemy. The fool, on the other hand, destroys that which is beautiful and lovely.

The fool speaks mischief (Proverbs 24:2). What else could come out of his mouth? It is out of the heart that the mouth speaks. The fool, having said in his heart there is no God, cannot help saying so with his lips. Many people attempt to compartmentalize the internal and external. They claim you can confess in your heart that there is no God while speaking wisdom with your lips. But God has not wired the world to work that way. While a God-denying man may speak a true sentence, that true sentence grew out of a heart that is ignorant of divine being and working at cross purposes with that divine being. God speaks words of life and blessing. The fool speaks diseased words: "Behold, the wicked man conceives evil and is pregnant with mischief and gives birth to lies" (Psalm 7:14).

The foolish man's mind cannot attain wisdom. Wisdom is on an entirely different plane—"Wisdom is too high for a fool" (Proverbs 24:7). The fool may know some things about the lower world. He might know how to make a buck and form an alliance. But bitterness, envy, and strife fuel his knowledge. He possesses the wisdom that is merely earthly (James 3:15). True wisdom comes from above. This heavenly wisdom *informs* earthly life. But it does not arise from earth. The foolish man, having no access to wisdom, has nothing to say when it matters. Proverbs 24:7 says, "In the gate he does not open his mouth." The gate of the city was the place of wise counsel. The decisions made there saved or destroyed the city and those inside its walls. We still have city gates at which the fool is silent. When your life begins to go to pieces, the fool knows not what to say. He lacks words when marriages are at the breaking point, children are troubled and afraid, nations gear up for war, and wolves stalk the church.

But the foolish man's ignorance does not stop him from planning. Adding trouble to trouble, the foolish man devises evil (Proverbs 24:8). The fool is dumb in one sense, but not in every sense. He comes up with exquisite strategies for destroying himself and others. The fool thinks his evil endeavors through. He charts a course, considers escape routes, secures plausible deniability, and identifies scapegoats. Beware of thinking a smart man is a wise man. The wise man knows how the things in the world work because he knows how the whole world works—he knows the creator of the world. The smart man knows how the things in the world work but without the knowledge of the whole, the heavenly, the purpose, and the Creator. Such a man ends up a schemer, attempting to use God's world against Him.

The end result of the fool's scheming is he turns himself into an abomination (Proverbs 24:9). In other words, he doesn't just make a few mistakes. You don't call a person who makes a few mistakes an abomination. An abomination is detestable, repulsive, and offensive. Mankind finds the abominable man odious. Such strong language makes certain people uneasy. Many have so exalted man that they deem *abomination* an inappropriate word. The prophet Jeremiah's words characterize us well: "Were they ashamed when they committed abomination? No, they were not at all ashamed; they did not know how to blush" (Jeremiah 8:12).

If Christians are going to build and fight well, then we need to take an account of how the fool builds and fights poorly. The wise man puts a fine point on the application: "Be not envious of evil men, nor desire to be with them" (Proverbs 24:1). We should be grateful that the fool is not the only one building. His story does not have to be our story.

The Wise Man Builds a House of Blessing

The wise man has what is necessary to build a house, for it is "by wisdom a house is built (Proverbs 24:3). Ravi Zacharias once told a story about visiting a university art hall that was quite proud of its postmodern outlook. Imagine leaning walls and staircases going nowhere. He remarked, "I bet you didn't do that stuff when you built the foundation." If you are going to build, then you must do so in step with the Creator. He establishes the principles down here. He created the materials you use to build. Building requires wisdom. This truth applies across the board. If you would build a city or a family, a business or a symphony, you need the wisdom that comes from God.

The wise man not only has what he needs to build a house but he also possesses what is necessary to *establish* a house (Proverbs 24:3). Establishment signals the need for endurance and perseverance. Understanding will not only help you get going, it will help you keep going. Trials will come. But Christians face those trials with minds informed by Christ's Word. As they do, Christ sanctifies them even through the challenges of establishing a house. Where you find a man established in his work, you find a man who has been through some things. The same goes for an established home, business, marriage, or any other good endeavor. The wise man has resources to navigate the difficulties of this world in a steady and fruitful way.

The wise man has what is necessary to fill a house—"By knowledge the rooms are filled with all precious and pleasant riches" (Proverbs 24:4). The Christian life is not an empty one. Too many people have been duped into thinking that Christianity is like plain, lukewarm oatmeal. It may be good for you, but there is not much flavor in there. That notion is exactly opposite of the truth. Life without God is the plain oatmeal. Life without God is the empty room. God created the earth, then told mankind to *fill it.* He gives us wisdom to fill the earth with good things, a house with good things, a life with good things.

How is this done? It is *by knowledge* that the rooms are filled. What kind of knowledge? In one sense, it is knowledge of all things. The wise man knows the Creator, so he knows the creation (the Creator's work). Christians know where everything has *come from*, and that includes everything from hammers to blue jays to football to Bach's "Toccata and Fugue in D minor, BWV565." They also know what everything *is for.* This knowledge helps them fill a life with precious things.

But the wise man possesses another knowledge. He knows redemption as well as creation. He has a special knowledge as well as a general knowledge. That special knowledge concerns wisdom Himself, the Son of God. The wise man knows Jesus Christ the righteous came into the world to save sinners. The wise man knows God's justice and mercy met on a hill called Calvary. He knows how to repent and believe.

To repent is to be sorry for sin, to hate and forsake it because it is displeasing to God. Repentance is not merely feeling sorry because we got caught. Getting caught is embarrassing. Getting caught can have real life consequences. But repentance is deeper than that. The repenting man cares about what God thinks. He loves God and sorrows because he has failed Him. Many do not have this knowledge of repentance. But such knowledge is essential to the very purpose of humanity. A man will never build and fight in the way he was designed to until he knows repentance.

In the same way, a man must know what it is to believe. This belief, or *faith*, is the other side of repentance. All repenting people believe, and all believing people repent. You can't have one without the other. Millions of people across the globe don't know what it is to believe in God. Sadly, they have never come to this saving knowledge. Faith is a knowledge, agreement, and personal trust in all God has said, particularly, trust in His Son, Jesus Christ, the Word made flesh for us and for our salvation. This saving knowledge of the Son is vital to a life of wisdom now and in the new heavens and new earth.

The wise man fills his house by this knowledge. But he also fills his house with "precious and pleasant riches" (Proverbs 24:4). Prosperity gospel preachers would hijack such a verse. They teach that you can fill your life with merely that which thieves steal and moths destroy. They miss the mark, but not by claiming that the precious and pleasant riches are real— some fall into the opposite ditch by teaching that the Christian's precious and pleasant riches are a dream, a wish, a cloudy hope with little to do with the here and now. That is not how our Christian forefathers lived. They went to the stake because their riches were so real and present.

The wise man's riches are so numerous they are hard to count. He enjoys the precious gift of being right with God. He enjoys the pleasant joy of the indwelling of the Spirit. He delights in his standing as an adopted son of God. He rejoices in the sanctifying work of Christ in him. He exults in his coming glorification. He lives in the kingdom of God, which is presently advancing throughout the world. He participates with Christ as he goes into all the world to make disciples, teaching them to observe all Christ has commanded.

The wise man does all this "full of strength" (Proverbs 24:5). He is far more than the stereotype of a man who can physically overpower others. The wise man possesses a strong mind informed by God's Word. He is strong in trials because he knows where they come from and what they are for. He endures loss as a reminder that he is not God and the Lord gives and takes away (Job 1:21). The wise man knows even how to find strength in his weakness, knowing that when he is weak, God is strong. The strength of the wise man is a full-orbed strength.

The wise man not only maintains strength but increases it (Proverbs 24:5). The foolish man will grow more foolish, and the wise man will grow wiser. The weak man will grow weaker, and the strong man will grow stronger. This is the logic of the kingdom of heaven. He who is faithful will be given more. He who is unfaithful will lose what he has, and it will be given to the faithful. This being the case, we should get after wisdom.

Wisdom teaches that "by wise guidance you can wage your war and in abundance of counselors there is victory" (Proverbs 24:6). The wise man then gathers other wise counselors to build and fight. Worldly thinking says, "I'm strong. I can figure this out on my own." Godly thinking says, "I'm strong. Let me gather wise counselors to guide me." The perennial temptation is to think we see the whole battlefield. We assume we have the bird's-eye view—the one God has. This is the mistake Adam and Eve made in the beginning when they desired to be like God. Truth be told, we are finite. We only see part of what is going on. Wise counselors will help us see more. With that knowledge, we can build a house of blessing.

Building in the Day of Adversity

As we prepare to build and fight, we must come to grips with adversity. There is no getting around resistance. When you plant a garden, weeds always need to be plucked and pests need to be poisoned. Everyone experiences the day of adversity. You are either in it or preparing for it. We shouldn't be surprised when the chain on our chainsaw snaps. And there's probably a pipe leaking in your walls right now. Whatever comes, we must not faint in the day of adversity (Proverbs 24:10). One good way not to faint in that day is to prepare for it. We do well to know it is coming.

People do faint in that day. That is why the wise man warns us not to faint. People cannot stand the heat, and so they get out of the kitchen. They cannot suffer the trials of being a Christian, so they quit. The apostle John tells us that they went out from us because they were not of us. Jesus Himself taught that many would receive the seed but for a little while and be scorched by the heat or choked by the weeds. The Christian life is an endurance race. We need not fear, for God will see all His children to the finish line. But that doesn't mean that we can quit the race. So, don't faint. Get strong. Get wisdom so you can endure the fiery trial when it comes upon you.

Staying on our feet is not the only goal either. Everybody here feels the sun's heat. Christians are to "rescue those who are being taken away to death" and "hold back those who are stumbling to the slaughter" (Proverbs 24:11). Doing this is hard. Assisting others who are going through adversity is costly. It will cost you time and money. It will cost you emotional ease. It will cost you prayers. It will cost you sleep. It will tax your family. It will cost you other pursuits. Those stumbling to the slaughter may not even be happy about your help. Folks who are about to die under the scorching heat may rather give up than press on. They just might get mad at you for coming alongside them with help. Given these dynamics, saving others in the day of adversity requires wisdom and genuine love. The fool has neither. The man who fears the Lord knows both.

Seeing how difficult the day of adversity is and considering how challenging it can be to rescue people being led away to death, it makes sense that people try to ignore this day and the people in it. Proverbs 24:12 addresses the problem of quitting. It addresses those who pretend like they didn't know and ignored the situation because they did not want to go through the trouble. It says, "If you say, 'Behold, we did not know this,' does not he who weighs the heart perceive it? Does not he who keeps watch over your soul know it, and will he not repay man according to his work?"

Do you see this temptation? "Oh, I did not know they were struggling." "Oh, I did not know things like this would happen." "Oh, I did not know that I was to prepare." God says those excuses won't work. He who weighs the heart knows the truth. The message is "Get knowledge and prepare for the day of adversity whether it be your own or belonging to someone else.

It is unspeakable glory that Jesus did not turn a blind eye to our plight. We made a mess of things. We brought adversity upon ourselves. He came as the building man, the fighting man, and endured in the day of distress. Adam gave way in the garden. Jesus sweat drops of blood in the garden. Adam fell asleep. Jesus stayed awake. Adam did his own will. Jesus did the will of the Father. We, now in Christ, have the resources to build and fight in stormy days.

13

CONCEALING SIN AND CONFESSING SIN

On the one hand, the idea that we would conceal sin is almost comical. God sees. What else matters? No sin is truly concealed. The most important being in the universe already knows. The sin we commit in the dark could not be more in the light in that sense. Then there is the cross. The cross says that we Christians were so wicked that the Son of God Himself had to die to save us. How silly that we would cover up our faults. The cross isn't covered up. Everybody already knows how bad we are.

But on the other hand, we can easily see why we hide our sin, like Moses covered up that dead body in the Egyptian desert. Exposed sin has particular kinds of consequences. Some of it has life-changing consequences. We do not want to face those changes, so we throw a blanket over our transgressions. If we brought forth the truth, we would face relational strain, public ridicule, financial loss, maybe even imprisonment. "Yeah, better to keep it between us and the Lord," we say. "I've confessed it to Him. He forgives me, right? No need to go public. Doesn't love cover a multitude of sins?"

Wisdom knows the difference between covering sin (1 Peter 4:8) and concealing sin (Proverbs 28:13). Love does the former. Folly does the latter—"whoever conceals his transgressions will not prosper, but he who confesses and forsakes them will obtain mercy" (Proverbs 28:13). That verse can unshackle men and women who are locked up in sin. Proverbs 28:13 is a liberty bell that rings with hope to those in the grip of Satan's tyranny. The devil hates confession. But heaven rejoices when a sinner repents.

Concealing Sin

Concealing sin is the pits. It is a sure-fire way to miss out on blessing. And we have been doing this for a long time.

We conceal our sin from God. Our first father, Adam, led the way. God put him in a garden where he could eat of any tree he wanted except one. After Adam and his wife ate the forbidden fruit, they "hid themselves from the presence of the LORD God among the trees of the garden" (Genesis 3:8). When we attempt to conceal our sin from God, what we end up doing is separating ourselves from Him. We may not hide among the trees as Adam did, but we hide in binge-watching, binge-drinking, binge-shopping, and pornography—anything to keep God away. The trees of the garden were not bad. Neither are God's good gifts in creation as we enjoy them according to His design. But when we use these "trees" to hide from God, we fall into the same trap our first parents did.

In doing so, we attempt to conceal our transgressions from ourselves. God has given human beings a conscience. He has set up the conscience as a little judge in the heart of man. But there is a way to have your conscience seared (1 Timothy 4:2). That searing is itself God's judgment. The apostle Paul says that God gives people up to their lusts, their dishonorable passions, and eventually to a "debased mind to do what ought not to be done" (Romans 1:28). If we get too good at concealing sin, we start to lose our grip on right and wrong, left and right, up and down. We begin to call good evil and evil good. We end up not knowing ourselves.

We lose genuine relationships with others too. We conceal sin from them. King David experienced this as he sinned against Uriah the Hittite. David should have confessed to stealing his wife. But he tried to hide that sin from Uriah. All David's avenues for concealment dried up, so he was left with murder as the only way of keeping his sin under wraps. A primary motivation for us hiding sin from one another is our pride. We simply want others to think well of us. We desire that glory that comes from man rather than the glory that comes from God.

There are three deadly costs for concealing sin. We lose relationship with God, with ourselves, and with others. But if we would leave off concealing sin, then we must notice the mechanics.

We conceal our transgressions by ignoring God's law. Sin is any transgression of the law of God. But if we pay little mind to God's law, we are in a much better position to conceal our sin. Here we have the inverse of the psalmist's wise words, "How can a young man keep his way pure? By guarding it according to your word" (Psalm 119:9). Without God's Word, we fall into that foolish and self-righteous trap of repenting over faux sin. We don't want to sorrow over our real sin, so we conjure up a fake one to lament. This is how many can advocate the slaughter of children in the womb while grieving in sackcloth and ashes over the harm our vehicles are doing to the environment. It is a scheme to keep the attention anywhere other than where it needs to be.

Sometimes we conceal our transgressions by acknowledging them but minimizing them. Yes, we said that slanderous word, but we did not really mean it. No, we have not treated God with the reverence He deserves, but who does? These are maneuvers—ones that do not lead to prospering.

No Prosperity

The wise man says that the man who conceals his sin will not prosper. Because we are dealing with the root of the matter, the lack of prospering runs in all directions. The point is not merely that we will lose out in one area of life. Rather, we end up losing everything. We come to the end with no fruit whatsoever.

We have seen this theme before. The wise man lives the good life. He rules as a king under the ultimate kingship of Jesus. He obeys the initial command from the Creator to be fruitful and multiply, fill the earth and subdue it. He has what it takes to fill a house, build a house, and meet the needs of the poor. But the one who conceals sin can do none of those things.

He does not prosper in relationship to God. He cannot pray as he ought. Prayer does not require perfection, but it does require honesty before God. If we conceal sin, our prayers become artificial. We begin to pretend that we are speaking to God rather than truly speaking to Him. We cannot sing as we ought. The joyful songs of the saints lose their luster. As Christians, we not only lift our voices to God but our very hearts. But the heart that conceals sin is weighed down and divided. We lose out as well on hearing from God. God speaks to His people. But there is a breakdown in communication when sin hides within the camp of the soul. This is what happened to Israel when Achan's sin was hidden in the camp. There would be no victory until the sin was brought to the light and dealt with. Christians enjoy the feast of the Lord's Supper. We commune with Christ and feed upon Him spiritually as we sit down at table with the Almighty. But the one who hides his sin does not prosper at the table. Paul tells us that people have gotten sick and even died by coming to the table in an inappropriate manner (1 Corinthians 11:30). A man's fellowship with the Spirit is also hindered as he paints over his sin. The Spirit is holy. He convicts us, sanctifies us, and helps us on to greater likeness to Christ. Our sweet communion with Him is troubled by sin concealed.

Without prosperity in relationship to God, a man will find he has no prosperity in other places either. His marriage stalls. The animating principle for marital love comes from the very love God has toward us, His grace at work within us. But concealed sin clogs up the operation, and the flow of this love suffers. He remains immature in his parenting as well. His children never see him repenting. They never see him growing. He cannot admit when he has missed the mark, so a dissonance settles into the family dynamics. The kids know things are not right, but the name of the game is pretending that they are. The Christian who conceals sin lacks blessing in the church as well. Fellowship with the saints goes through malnutrition. He does not say with David, "As for the saints in the land, they are the excellent ones, in whom is all my delight" (Psalm 16:3).

Concealed sin not only stunts growth in relationship to God and others but the man himself lacks maturity. His mind does not prosper. He begins to lose his grip on the truth. His heart grows cold, unable to feel as it did before. His strength is dried up, for the joy of the Lord that was his strength now runs at a low ebb. His daily work becomes mere drudgery. He no longer sees his vocation as a labor that glorifies God and serves others. He turns in on himself, thinking less and less of others. It makes sense that the wise man teaches that "the way of the transgressors is hard" (Proverbs 13:15 KJV).

The good news is that things don't have to be this way. There is another route to take. That route is the pathway of confession.

CONFESSING AND FORSAKING

Christians confess their sin, which they do by the power of the Holy Spirit. The unbelieving do not know how to confess their sin. They can downplay it, ignore it, suppress it, or justify it, but they cannot simply name it for what it is. We can't be honest about ourselves without the cross.

There is, however, the danger of stopping short of true confession. Human beings become masterful at the "I'm sorry, but..." That sort of confession won't do. What is the nature of true confession?[6]

First, he who confesses his transgressions sees his sin. When hunting a deer, it is terribly difficult to kill it if you can't see it. The same is true for killing sin. We identify sin by examining our lives according to God's law. People get into all sorts of trouble when they name sin without God's law. We end up falsely accusing others; we end up falsely accusing ourselves. Seeing our sin includes seeing the gravity of it. Isaiah saw how unclean he was when he saw the Lord high and lifted up. Without an apprehension of the majesty of God and glory of His Son crucified and risen for us, our sin will appear smaller than it really is.

Along with seeing our sin we must also confesses the heart behind the sin. It can be quite humorous to watch how we like to chop ourselves up into parts when confessing sin. Adam said it was the woman God gave him. We can blame the hands God gave us, the eyes God gave us, the tongues God gave us—anything but the heart. Yet we operate from the inside out. The heart moves, and then we move. Our sin, while not restricted to our heart, does spring forth from the inside. Thus, we should not blame our parts when we err but own our sin all the way down.

As we do, we should sorrow over our sin—which is different than wallowing in it. Sin is a monster. It does damage. It strikes at God Himself and harms those made in His image. Once we have the sin in view, we should come to grips with its true nature and consequences, lamenting what we have done appropriately. The apostle Paul rejoiced that his fellow Christians were grieved into repenting. So, let there be grief in your repentance seasoned with joy that we are grieved over our sin.

Shame should accompany our confession and repentance too. Modern man retracts in horror at the thought of being ashamed. Christians do not. We are not ashamed at all of the gospel of Jesus Christ, but we are ashamed when we sin against our Christ. Our shame is not the shame of one who bears his guilt outside of Christ. Rather, we have the shame sons and daughters experience when they sin against their father. This is a shame that Christ bears with us and raises us up out of, but it is a shame nonetheless. Second Thessalonians 3:14 says, "If anyone does not obey what we say in this letter, take note of that person, and have nothing to do with him, that he may be ashamed." God, through the prophet Jeremiah, warns of sin without shame when he says, "They have healed the wound of my people lightly, saying, 'Peace, peace,' when there is no peace. Were they ashamed when they committed abomination? No, they were not at all ashamed; they did not know how to blush" (Jeremiah 6:14–15).

True confession contains within it a hatred for sin. That is why Paul can speak of putting "to death the deeds of the body" (Romans 8:13). We kill it because we hate it. We hate it because it dishonors the holy God who loves us.

It follows that genuine confession results in forsaking sin. While we will not obtain perfection in this life, Christians do experience real change. We "bear fruits in keeping with repentance" (Luke 3:8). We are known by that fruit (Matthew 7:15–20). Jesus has no problem confronting those who say one thing but do the opposite. He asks, "Why do you call me 'Lord, Lord,' and not do what I tell you?" (Luke 6:46). The apostle John calls this walking in the light (1 John 1:5–10). We plod on, leaving the old man behind. We make progress, putting on the new man.

OBTAINING MERCY

Those who confess sin obtain mercy. What a lovely promise to move us toward repentance. The repenting man receives the tender affection and compassion of God. He will know God's fatherly affection. The mercies received by repenting Christians are manifold.

They obtain the mercy of not continuing in sin. Walking in darkness isn't really a great idea in the first place. You tend to run into things when you do. Sinners who go on in their sin find themselves in just that situation. But the one who leaves off his sin knows the joy of walking in the light. He knows where he is going. He knows whom he is with.

The repenting man knows the mercy of having Christians pray for him. If sin is concealed, then the saints don't know about it. God knows, but the saints are left in the dark. They cannot pray for strength in that situation. But when sin is brought to the light, brothers and sisters go to praying. God hears and answers, and things start to get better.

The confessing man gets the mercy of facing sin's consequences. When we are not thinking right, this does not feel like a mercy. It is the very thing we were trying to avoid by burying our sin underground. But God disciplines those whom He loves. He does not condemn, but He corrects through consequences that work for our good and His glory.

The mercies received through confession are good. But things only get sweeter as we see these mercies are never-ending. Lamentations 3:21–22 says, "But this I call to mind, and therefore I have hope: The steadfast love of the LORD never ceases; his mercies never come to an end." The sorrow and pain involved in owning up to what we have done cannot compare to the rich mercy we will receive day after day without end.

This never-ending mercy involves having God as our portion—"'The LORD is my portion,' says my soul" (Lamentations 3:24). We end up having God Himself, which is incomparable to having our sin. We know His goodness and steadfast love.

A final mercy received by repenting is humility. The man with sin concealed tries to fool others and himself. He thinks he is much more than what he is. But the man who owns what he has done before God truly knows himself. He can look at himself with right judgment. He knows what it is to walk humbly with God, happy to simply be called a son and call God Father. He is content with His Father's love and confident of His never-ceasing fatherly affection.

REPENTING ROYALTY

To be a son or daughter of the Most High is to be a king or queen. He tells us to rule. But a temptation comes in when we begin to rule. We think we must be perfect. We have to have everything together. That is not what kings and queens do. That is what God does. And we are not Him.

We are, however, a city on a hill, a light in the darkness, lights that shine amid a crooked and twisted generation. The way to pollute the darkness without being polluted by the darkness is to confess sin and forsake it. We do this in view of the true King, the King of Kings. His name is Jesus Christ. Trust Him. Confess sin. You will obtain mercy.

14

THE WOMAN WHO FEARS THE LORD

There is an intimate connection between the fear of the Lord and true womanhood. When the fear of the Lord is up, true womanhood is up. When the fear of the Lord is down, so goes true womanhood. We live in quite godless times, so womanhood is not exactly flourishing.

The decline of womanhood in our society has a detailed history. It has mirrored the rise of feminism. When feminism goes up, womanhood goes down. When womanhood goes up, feminism goes down. The first wave of feminism arose in the United States in the nineteenth century. In an effort to get women the right to vote, Elizabeth Cady Stanton cut Genesis 2 and 3 out of the Bible. She wrote,

> The whole foundation of the Christian religion rests on the woman's temptation and man's fall, hence the necessity of a Redeemer and a plan of salvation. . . . Woman's degradation and subordination were made a necessity. If, however, we accept the Darwinian theory,

that the race has been a gradual growth from the lower to a higher form of life, and that the story of the fall is a myth, we can exonerate the snake, emancipate the woman, and reconstruct a more rational religion.[7]

The shoe fits. Feminism has a way of getting people to act like monkeys in the name of emancipating women. Margaret Sanger was another influential leader in this first wave of feminism. She founded the organization that would come to be Planned Parenthood, which in the name of women's empowerment slaughters thousands of women every year.

Kate Millett was a leader in the second wave of feminism in America. She was a homosexual woman who wrote books and held meetings in which the following call and response was heralded:

"Why are we here today?" she asked.

"To make revolution," [the group] answered.

"What kind of revolution?" she replied.

"The Cultural Revolution," they chanted.

"And how do we make Cultural Revolution?" she demanded.

"By destroying the American family!" they answered.

"How do we destroy the family?" she came back.

"By destroying the American Patriarch," they cried exuberantly.

"And how do we destroy the American Patriarch?" she replied.

"By taking away his power!"

"How do we do that?"

"By destroying monogamy!" they shouted.

"How can we destroy monogamy?" . . .

"By promoting promiscuity, eroticism, prostitution, and homosexuality!"[8]

They were shrewd. They were right. They were successful. So if a godly woman starts helping her husband, which is what she was created to do, you can see that she's going to get steamrolled by feminists. Laws were established in the '60s and '70s, including Roe v. Wade, which effectively separated the idea of womanhood from household, family, and nurturing.

A third wave of feminism is upon us. It has made inroads into the evangelical world. Feminism, while increasingly coming into conflict with dimensions of the LGBT movement, nevertheless partners with it in an effort to erase the image of God in man and woman.

Why is this history important? Because every one of us has grown up in this climate. The temperature has been increased slowly. We don't realize how hot the boiling water is in this pot. If Christian women live as women who fear the Lord, they will be ridiculed by this world. They will be persecuted in a particular way because of our particular moment and this particular feminist movement. It is helpful to know what they have been up to as they mock Christian women. The godly women who are into their husbands and their children and busy caring for their households are not the crazy ones. They are not the ones throwing prostitutes at their husbands and claiming we all came from chimpanzees.

Biblical womanhood is far too precious a thing to be clouded and disregarded by the perversion of our present moment. Into our mess and our sexually disorienting times comes God's kind and wise words. He supplies a glorious picture of the woman who fears the Lord in Proverbs 31. It is every Christian woman's responsibility to grow up into this woman. And it is every Christian man's responsibility to suffer and die to see that his wife, daughters, mother, and Christian sisters become more and more like this woman.

The picture is an ideal one. Some have concluded that the passage ought not to be taught plainly. They fear such a glorious picture would inevitably result in women condemning themselves for not measuring up. Those who make such a mistake have far too low a view of Christian women and the Christ who saves and sanctifies them. Not one of us measures up to what we should be, man or woman. But being clothed in the righteousness of Christ, we labor to be perfect as our heavenly Father is perfect.

So, we don't use the image as an instrument of condemnation. But we do use it as a guide as women are transformed from one degree of glory to another. Such a transformation is worth it. The woman who fears the Lord reaps the fruit of her diligent labor for the Lord. The most central thing about her is that she fears the Lord. This being the case, she happily goes about a flurry of work for Him. As she does, she reaps what she sows and enjoys the fat and rich rewards of all her faith-filled work.

We have two truths before us about this lady who fears the Lord. First comes the truth about her happy labor. Second, we see her joyful reaping.

Her Happy Labor

Proverbs 31 explodes a common erroneous idea about woman. Let's call it the "woman is just a…" fallacy. She just has a little slice of the pie. She is just a wife, just a mom, just a homemaker. Feminists employed this lie hard against housewives in the '60s. But the woman's work is extensive. Did you notice all that she does (Proverbs 31:10–31)? She's a homemaker, clothes designer, chef, educator, manager in the human resources department, and philanthropist. She is into real estate, agriculture, fabrics, sales, and market analysis.

She does all this *happily*. Verse 13 says, "[She] works with willing hands." In Hebrews 13:17, elders must labor over the flock with joy, and if there is no joy, then there is no benefit to the flock. Likewise, the woman must labor with a song. If her heart is not singing, she's not doing it right and won't get the fruit in the end.

Before we look at her labor, I should mention there are always unique circumstances. A woman may be physically unable to do some of this labor. She may not have a husband. She may not have children. Some may not have a home. But in the main, this is the godly woman's labor.

First, she helps her husband. Verse 11 says, "He will have no lack of gain." Verse 12 adds, "She does him good, and not harm, all the days of her life." He profits from her in demonstrable ways. This can be intimidating. As long as it is only the idea of helping we're talking about, which cannot be measured, we're comfortable. But the text tells us she does him genuine good. Her benefit to him touches on a number of areas, like his relationship to God, his morality and character, his financial resources, his sexual satisfaction, his work life, and more. One of many ways in which she does this is by not being a doormat. She speaks the truth to her husband, and in so doing, does him good. Verse 23 says this godly woman's "husband is known in the gates when he sits among the elders of the land." He sits at the place of wisdom and counsel, where he can be a blessing to others. His good wife has helped him get there.

The godly woman keeps her house. Verse 27 says, "She looks well to the ways of her household and does not eat the bread of idleness." The decline of womanhood is seen in the decline of home economics. Today many people live in disorder and stress in their homes because this principle is neglected. First Timothy 5:14 speaks of women as managers of their households. There is nothing demeaning about that station. It is a glorious one. Paul's language is strong. She reigns over a domain. That means if she says to her husband, "Dirty clothes are to go in the hamper, dear," then he should gladly put them in the hamper. Yes, man is the head of woman, but a man ought not get in his wife's way when she's doing her thing for the Lord in the home. She's got biblical warrant to be the keeper of the house. Moreover, her keeping the home does not mean she is the only one working in the home. Children are to listen to their mother's law. And that includes them doing the dishes.

She shops well. Verse 14 says, "She is like the ships of the merchant; she brings her food from afar." That means Sam's Club runs. Take heart, anxious wives headed to the supermarket, women have been doing this kind of thing for generations. It has its challenges indeed. I cannot think of many godly works that are more underappreciated, foolishly so. When you find anyone minimizing grocery shopping, just tell them to go a few days without using the items found there. Shopping should not be done frivolously. There are scams abroad at the supermarket. Some ladies do this well. Some ladies do not. But this, too, can and ought to be learned. Men, don't expect your wives to go bring home food if you're not resourcing them to do so. If she is full of anxiety about the bill every week, it is up to you to fix that problem through encouragement, wisdom, and resources.

She feeds her family. Verse 15 says, "She rises while it is yet night and provides food for her household and portions for her maidens." She doesn't cook up something just for the Instagram photo. She's not in it for the likes of others online. She rather cooks a fitting meal for her household, something that complements a thankful husband, children, neighbors, and friends as they gather around for fellowship and nourishment. Family table time has fallen on hard times. You don't get the sense that food is eaten in a big rush out the door in this woman's home. She prepares a table. She provides a place for the household to sit and talk about God and His ways. Godly women fan into flame the joy of the family by the hard and happy work of providing food for them to enjoy together.

This woman dresses herself and her household nicely. Verse 13 says, "She seeks wool and flax, and works with willing hands." Verse 22 continues, "She makes bed coverings for herself; her clothing is fine linen and purple." When Peter says that a woman's adorning should not be external (1 Peter 3:3), he does not mean that she should let herself go. He means that she shouldn't be more focused on externals than she is on internals. She should care about the heart, which will express itself externally. First Timothy 2:9 says, "Women should adorn themselves in respectable apparel." She should have dignity within which expresses itself in dignified clothing.

She is a theologically educated teacher. Verse 26 says, "She opens her mouth with wisdom, and the teaching of kindness is on her tongue." She does not snap at the household with her tongue. She does not feed anxiety, worry, and despair with her tongue. It is the teaching of kindness that is on her tongue. Where does she get this wisdom? Study. She reads. She seeks the truth. Women are to learn. It is a foolish man who thinks that women should not be educated. This is why we raise our girls to learn the laundry and Latin. For some odd reason, people nowadays think those two things are unrelated. But the woman who keeps a house also keeps a library. She teaches Bible studies and children, writes books, publishes podcasts, takes courses, and so on.

She nurtures the poor. Verse 20 says, "She open her hand to the poor and reaches out her hands to the needy." The woman who fears the Lord has worked so diligently, she has goods to give to the needy. She compassionately produces so much fruit, she has fruit to share.

With the fruit of her hands she nurtures the world at a profit to her household. We see her doing this in several texts. Verse 16 says, "She considers a field and buys it; with the fruit of her hands she plants a vineyard." Verse 18 says, "She perceives that her merchandise is profitable. Her lamp does not go out at night." Verse 19 adds, "She puts her hands to the distaff, and her hands hold the spindle." And verse 24 concludes, "She makes linen garments and sells them; she delivers sashes to the merchant." There is a bad idea out there that says the true woman works only in the home. She is boxed up to that one little spot, producing no impact on the world around her. That is not an accurate picture. Rather, home is her headquarters from which she attacks the world for Christ, makes advancements for Christ in the world. This does not require that she has some form of financial employment. The woman who provides a second income is not necessarily fulfilling this principle (though she may be). The point is that this lady has the same orientation to the world Eve had as she labored with her husband to fill the earth, subdue it, and exercise dominion over it.

But notice she nurtures the world at a profit to her household, not at a loss to her household. There is the woman who, having a surplus, nourishes the world. Then there is the woman who, lacking that surplus, nourishes neither because she has put world and the home in the wrong order. Wicked men will speak all about a woman's empowerment in order to get her to neglect her household. The husband permits this for a variety of reasons. But the family gets sacrificed along with the principles in Proverbs 31.

We are susceptible to manipulation on this point because we have been taught to think of a woman's home life as disconnected from her world and work life. But the same wool and flax the Proverbs 31 woman gets for her household goes to the needy and the merchants. So, the vision is from household to the world: the godly woman provides food for her household and then from the surplus feeds the needy or opens the bakery. She provides clothes for her family, and then from the extra she launches the online store. She educates her children unto the writing of books for others or the opening of the bookstore. She weeds her own garden then purchases more acreage to farm. She plays the piano for her family's enjoyment, which blossoms into making the album for others. She nurses her children unto the nursing of others. She studies God's Word for her own edification, which spreads to the discipling of others.

So home is not first base that she eagerly tries to get past in order to get to the second base. Rather, she is a fruitful woman who richly supplies her family to the spilling over of richly supplying the world.

Her Joyful Reaping

The woman who fears the Lord not only labors with a Isaiah, she reaps with one too. She's living the good life. She's living the way God intended and enjoys the produce of God's good world.

First, she reaps a life of great value. Verse 10 says, "An excellent wife who can find? She is far more precious than jewels." She really is a rare thing, especially in our day. The man who finds a wife like this finds more than a good thing. It is a tragedy of our times that little girls mostly have secular idols. Christian parents must not pretend that the crop-topped princess is the girl who is really "sucking the marrow out of life." She's not. She's not more precious than jewels. Find ways to lift up and hold forth godly women who happily labor for Christ the way this lady in Proverbs 31 does.

Second, she reaps the trust of her husband. Verse 11 says, "The heart of her husband trusts in her." He trusts her because she is trustworthy, not because of some highly romanticized, sentimental narrative that says trust flowers in every marriage. It does not. Trust is built brick by brick. This godly woman has built a credible home on a foundation of faithfulness. When a woman has demonstrably improved her husband's life in the ways described, he trusts her, she knows he trusts her, and the kids know he trusts her. That knowledge makes her happy.

Third, she reaps true strength. Verse 17 says, "She dresses herself with strength and makes her arms strong." The world has a lot to say about women's strength. Their message usually sounds forth from a lady who is scantily clad on a stage or screen. She sings about how independently strong she is, while perverted men cheer her on. The message is "Neglect your household, and do what I do. Then you will be strong." When translated, that actually means, "I know you're tired from all your labor for the Lord, so come join me in being weak and lazy." Meanwhile, the women who fear the Lord plod on working with their hands and hearts. They are models of true strength. Young ladies, don't be sold a bill of goods. These false narratives abound at every turn. Find the woman who is doing the things marked out in Proverbs 31, and follow her example.

Fourth, she reaps fearlessness. Verse 21 says, "She is not afraid of snow for her household, for all her household are clothed in scarlet." She is not a fretful woman. She is not anxiety-ridden. She remembers that the Lord is at hand. She remembers God is her rock and her refuge. She is like the holy women of old who hoped in God and therefore did not fear what was frightening. How do you not fear something that is frightening? How do you not fear the children's futures? Sickness? Financial constraint? Housework? The answer is *you fear the Lord*. The woman who fears the Lord is fearless.

Fifth, she reaps a joyful gaze to the future. Verse 25 says, "Strength and dignity are her clothing, and she laughs at the time to come." She's a happy warrior. She's a glad builder. She's not frantically working while looking at the gathering storm. This woman looks at next week's schedule and laughs. She sees the events of the next few months and rejoices in her God who is faithful. (She also knows when to say no and when to make changes to that schedule given genuine limitations). She understands that for the Christian, the best is always yet to come. God calls us further up and further in to His glory and goodness. King Jesus reigns both in heaven and down here where we shed blood, sweat, and tears working with sore backs and hands. She is not free of all struggle and pain. But she laughs through it with eyes full of hope set on the kingdom of Christ.

Sixth, she reaps the praise of her family and others. Verse 28 says, "Her children rise up and call her blessed; her husband also, and he praises her:

'Many women have done excellently, but you surpass them all.'" Verse 31 says, "Give her of the fruit of her hands, and let her works praise her in the gates." One of the tactics of our enemy is to get us thinking we will not reap a harvest. If you can get your opponents to doubt the harvest, you can get them to stop sowing. But Proverbs teaches us again and again that God established this world in wisdom. When we live according to His wisdom, good things happen. Fruit happens. "Let us not grow weary of doing good, for in due season we will reap, if we do not give up" (Galatians 6:9). This woman who fears the Lord will get the fruit of her hands. It is coming to her.

Conclusion

This godly woman happily labors for the Lord and reaps the fruit of her hard work. But I want to conclude by thinking about where her energy comes from. The answer is found in verse 30, "Charm is deceitful, and beauty is vain, but a woman who fears the LORD is to be praised." Again, this does not mean that women avoid beauty or pursue ugliness. It means this woman is not overly concerned with appearances, how things look on the outside to the eyes of others. She is rather concerned first and foremost with the heart, ensuring she fears the Lord. She reverences God. She loves Christ. She depends on the Spirit. The woman who humbles herself, turning in faith and devotion to obey her God and Father, finds fresh and inexhaustible supplies for working for the LORD in this world.

Where can she find this reverence, this fear of the Lord? *Christ.* She must go often to Christ. Remember Him. Trust Him. Call out to Him. Rejoice in Him. Remember that He is the only one who has lived perfectly out of reverence and love for His Father.

Christ is the one who humbled Himself to magnify the Father. He looked to the ways of His household, ensuring that all the children came in and got washed. He came from heaven like the merchant ships, bringing true bread to nourish us. He satisfies us as with fat and rich food. He has dressed the family of God in the finest of clothes, having provided us with His very own righteousness. He has taught us wisdom with kindness on his tongue. He opened His hand to the poor and proclaimed good news to them. Out of His abounding grace, He has lavished blessing upon the world at a profit to His chosen people.

Christian women magnify Him as they labor for the Lord. They do what He did as they follow His example. They find strength to do so by going to Him as provider, helper, Lord, and Savior.

Friends here who don't know Christ savingly, you have in the picture of this godly woman a picture of Christ. He has provided salvation for His people through His life, death, and resurrection. He is the Son of God who became man in order to save sinners like you and me. Trust Him, turning away from your sins, and you will be saved. You will join the ranks of those who fear the Lord, work happily for Him, and receive the fruit of their hands.

15

THE FEAR OF THE LORD

Jordan Peterson is a Canadian professor of psychology at the University of Toronto. He is an intriguing figure who has much appreciation for Judeo-Christian thought. Interestingly, when asked if he believes in God, after pondering it for a moment, he said, "Well, I live as if God exists." In a recent lecture he was admiring an engraving of Moses with the Ten Commandments and said to his audience,

> Break the law and see what happens. Break the universal moral law, man, and see what happens. . . . I see people like this all the time because I'm a clinical psychologist. If the people I'm seeing have not broken the universal moral law, then you can be sure the people around them have. It's no joke. Like, you make a mistake and things will go seriously wrong for you. . . . Stay awake, speak properly, be honest, or watch out because things will come your way that you just do not want to see at all. . . . Most people know that deep in their hearts.

That's why the Old Testament says, "The fear of God is the beginning of wisdom." You can't twist the fabric of reality without having it snap back. It doesn't work that way. Why would it? Because what are you going to do? Twist the fabric of reality? I don't think so. I think it's bigger than you. And one of the things that really tempts people is the idea that "Well, I can get away with it." It's like, yeah, you try, see how well that works. You get away with nothing. And that's the beginning of wisdom. And it's something that deeply terrifies me. Look out, man, 'cause there are rules. And if you break them, God help you[9].

Peterson understands this fundamental truth about the world: we don't make up the rules. They have been placed on us. We do not break the rules but break ourselves against them. He has drawn an accurate connection between that truth and the fear of the Lord. Proverbs 9:10 says, "The fear of the Lord is the beginning of wisdom, and the knowledge of the Holy One is insight."

If you would live well, you must have the fear of the Lord. People want to live well. You can tell that by the size of the self-help section at the bookstore. We have titles such as *5 Ways to Lose Weight and Gain Friends* and *The Secret Art of Raising Happy Children*.

But we don't go far enough. We try, but we slip off the path of the well-lived life because we don't fear God. We need more than a strategy, tips and tricks, a schedule, a routine, self-control. There's nothing wrong with these things. They are instrumental in living a well-ordered, happy life. But if we do not have the fear of the Lord, everything falls flat.

The fear of the Lord is the reverence a child of God has for his Father that moves him to humbly obey God's law. The well-lived life is the wisely lived life. It is life in accordance with God's wisely established laws. The only way to walk on that wise pathway is to have reverence for God. The only way to rule as kings and queens for Christ is to fear the Lord. In this last chapter, I will point to nine truths about fearing God.

NINE TRUTHS ABOUT FEARING GOD

First, the fear of the Lord is the beginning of knowledge. You cannot get knowledge without the fear of God. We have all experienced trying to teach a stubborn, prideful person something. It's frustrating. You have a simple truth. You know it is true. It's a verifiable fact. Yet, you cannot seem to get your puffed-up listener to receive it. He cannot accept it. He cannot assimilate it as knowledge because he lacks humility.

The fear of the Lord provides the ability to gain knowledge. We cannot truly know reality without knowing the God who made it. We do not make our own reality, as certain philosophers have taught. Rather, we come to know what is real through the fear of God. This world has a creator. He sustains the world. His name is Jesus Christ. Hebrews 1:3 says, "He upholds the universe by the word of his power." Natural laws stay the same because He stays the same. And if we would gain knowledge about natural law, moral law, the physical world, the spiritual world, or any other type of reality you can think of, we must fear the creator and sustainer of that reality.

Second, the pressure is on to choose the fear of the Lord. It is not as if you can get away with ignorance. The fear of God is not something that can be put on the back burner. It doesn't work like that. The clock is ticking. Reality is coming at you. You will reap what you sow for good or bad. Remember, wisdom has warned, "Then they will call upon me, but I will not answer; they will seek me diligently but will not find me. Because they hated knowledge and did not choose the fear of the LORD, would have none of my counsel and despised all my reproof, therefore they shall eat the fruit of their way, and have their fill of their own devices" (Proverbs 1:28–31).

This is a great temptation for young people. In the early season of life, you think, "I have time. I can make a few mistakes. My parents did." But that is a lie. You don't have time. The decisions you make today will bear fruit. You think you have time because you don't see the bad fruit immediately. But the seed is sown, and it will come forth one day. Truth is like this lady. If you turn your back on her now, she will laugh at your pain when it comes home to roost.

Third, obtaining the fear of the Lord requires great effort. Getting the fear of the Lord is not like turning on a light switch and getting light. Indeed, we are born again in a moment. We go from the kingdom of darkness to the kingdom of light in a given moment. But the fear of the Lord must be cultivated. Proverbs 2:1–5 says, "My son, *if you receive my words* and treasure up my commandments with you, making your ear attentive to wisdom and inclining your heart to understanding; yes, if you call out for insight and raise your voice for understanding, if you seek it like silver and search for it as for hidden treasures, *then you will understand the fear of the* LORD and find the knowledge of God."

The "if-then" structure of this passage is inescapable. If you would fear God, then you must receive the truth. You must pay attention. You must love the truth, treasuring up God's commands. You must cry out for the truth. If you're not hungry for the truth of God, then you're not going to get the fear of God. That's why Christ taught us to pray, "Our Father in heaven, hallowed be your name." We need help for this work. God gives strength for this labor as we call out to Him in prayer.

The pursuit of the fear of the Lord is not merely an endeavor for really smart people. If you think of it that way, you will be tempted to say, "That study stuff is just not for me." But every child of God should be cultivating this hunger for wisdom and the fear of God. If Jesus Himself is the truth, then every one of His followers are called to the hard work of seeking Him. We press on to know Him more and more that we might fear God.

Fourth, obtaining the fear of the Lord requires humbly listening to instruction. We must take great care to listen. There is a type of person who boasts very much in his hard work, perhaps even his hard study, but is working hard in the wrong direction. He is working hard in one way and outright lazy in the way that counts.

Proverbs 15:33 says, "The fear of the LORD is instruction in wisdom, and humility comes before honor." The fear of God is tied to instruction in wisdom. Jesus Christ is the Word made flesh. He dwelt among us to show us the truth. If we would fear God, we must learn from Christ. We must listen to Christ, "in whom are hidden all the treasures of wisdom and knowledge" (Colossians 2:3). The apostle Paul says in 2 Corinthians 10:5, "We destroy arguments and every lofty opinion raised against the knowledge of God, and take every thought captive to obey Christ." Christ instructs all our thoughts. In Him is found *all* wisdom. We must rid ourselves of the division between the sacred and secular. All belongs to Christ.

The point is not to stop living and working in the world to read books. The point is rather to live your life and do your work, whatever it is, knowledgeably. Live and work in the knowledge of Christ. Think all your thoughts, whatever subject is being considered, in the fear of God and wisdom of Christ.

Fifth, the fear of the Lord yields life. Proverbs drives this point home repeatedly. Proverbs 10:27 says, "The fear of the LORD *prolongs life*, but the years of the wicked will be short." Proverbs 14:27 tells us, "The fear of the LORD is *a fountain of life*, that one may turn away from the snares of death." Proverbs 19:23 says, "The fear of the LORD *leads to life*, and whoever has it rests satisfied; he will not be visited by harm." Proverbs 22:4 declares, "The reward for humility and fear of the LORD is *riches and honor and life*."

If you get the fear of God, then you will enjoy life in this body and in the resurrected body. The devil has been running this play on mankind for some time. He lied to Eve about the good life. He told her that God set a limit for her so that she would miss out. She believed the Serpent. She ate. She suffered. Don't be fooled like she was. Adam and Eve are an example for us so that we would not be duped by the devil.

Why would we think that obedience to the good laws of the all-wise God wouldn't be good? Would we really want to go our own way with our little pea-brains? Do we think that things would work out better for us if we, rather than the one who made the forest, were holding the compass? Do we really want to try to take the compass out of His hand? Scripture says the way of the transgressor is hard, and the sorrows of those who run after other gods shall multiply (Proverbs 13:15; Psalm 16:4). But the Lord is our portion (Psalm 119:57). And the lines have fallen in pleasant places for us (Psalm 16:6). Our souls will be satisfied with fat and rich food as we trust God and keep His commandments.

But how challenging it is to do so. If you get serious about following God's way, you are going to run up against numerous people who hate you. For "all who desire to live a godly life in Christ Jesus will be persecuted" (2 Timothy 3:12).

Sixth, the fear of the Lord fuels courage. Everyone wants to be courageous, but there are a lot of pitfalls. On the one hand, you can aim at courage and just hit arrogance. You do what Grandma used to call "getting too big for your britches." Pride comes before a fall. On the other hand, you can just be a coward, shrinking back from the scary things in life. Proverbs 14:26 is a sure guide. It says, "In the fear of the LORD one has strong confidence, and his children will have a refuge." In the fear of the Lord a man avoids the first danger because he reveres God. He's humbled himself before God.

Such a man also avoids cowardice because if you fear God, then you don't fear anything else. Each person is left to one of these fears or the other. You will either fear God and nothing else, or you won't fear God and thus fear everything else. One of these will exist in your heart—the fear of God or the fear of man. It is not whether you will fear but whom you will fear.

We live in a scary place. There are all sorts of tragedies out there. We will know trials and tribulations. Loss is coming. Death is coming. Pain is coming. Sickness is coming. Sin crouches at the door. What are you going to do in the face of all these frightening things? The answer must be fear God and laugh at the days to come. That is the only way to go forward with courage.

Seventh, the fear of the Lord helps us be less greedy. Every one of us knows what it is like to be greedy. We see it so clearly in children because they haven't learned how to be as sneaky about it. But we want the piece of cake on the other person's plate too. How do you remedy that? Pretending like you don't want your neighbor's cake, house, and wife isn't the solution. God sees the heart. The solution? Fear God.

Proverbs 23:17 says, "Let not your heart envy sinners, but continue in the fear of the LORD all the day." The solution to envy is the fear of the Lord. One of these two will reside within—the envy of sinners or the fear of God. If you fear God, then you know that those who sin against His law will suffer the consequences. Such a man does not envy sinners but pities them.

Likewise, Proverbs 15:16 says, "Better is a little with the fear of the LORD than great treasure and trouble with it." It is amazing how quickly we can go after great treasure and how quickly we can justify our greedy underhanded pursuit of it. Beware, for while there is nothing wrong with working hard and enjoying and sharing the fruits of our labor, "those who desire to be rich fall into temptation, into a snare, into many senseless and harmful desires that plunge people into ruin and destruction" (1 Timothy 6:9).

Eighth, those who fear God hate evil. Hate is a Christian duty. Many have allowed their hatred of evil to cool off. Others have fallen into the trap of hating the wrong things or hating as the world does—without faith. We have become far too comfortable with the evil around us. But the root cause of all our peace treaties with sin is that we just don't fear God. We instead fear what man would say about us if we testified the truth about wickedness. Proverbs 8:13 says, "The fear of the LORD is hatred of evil. Pride and arrogance and the way of evil and perverted speech I hate."

Many Christians have not considered that they should hate more. Saying so will indeed get you some strange looks. But God is angry with the wicked every day (Psalm 7:11). He tells us plainly in the New Testament to hate what is evil (Romans 12:9). We should hate the perversion of sexuality. We should hate the slaughter of children in the womb. We should hate the use and abuse of women by male leaders. We should hate filthy and corrupt speech and many other things.

But we shouldn't just hate evil at a distance. We must, first and foremost, hate it within our own flesh. Proverbs 16:6 says, "By steadfast love and faithfulness iniquity is atoned for, and by the fear of the LORD one turns away from evil." We should hate evil so deeply that we turn away from it in disgust. We should hate with a hatred that causes us to take up the sword of the Spirit and put it to death.

Ninth, those who fear the Lord walk uprightly. They will hate evil *and* walk uprightly. These two are inseparable. Proverbs 14:2 says, "Whoever walks in uprightness fears the LORD, but he who is devious in his ways despises him." The fear of the Lord is not merely a feeling. Neither is it not less than a feeling. Genuine reverence must reside in the heart of one who fears the Lord. Any attempt to obey God's commands without reverence for Him falls short. But genuine affection for God must manifest itself in our lives. We don't get to say we fear Him while running roughshod over His commandments. The fear of God straightens a man up. It sends him walking in accordance with God's statutes. The Preacher tells us, "The end of the matter; all has been heard. Fear God and keep his commandments, for this is the whole duty of man" (Ecclesiastes 12:13).

How to Get the Fear of God

If you would live well, then you must have the fear of the Lord. That's what Proverbs teaches us about the fear of God. But how do we obtain this fear, keep it, live in it? It is a slippery thing. We may do well for a little while. We can stay humble for a few hours. But when we slip up—and we do slip up—we're left breaking God's rules.

Well, God has helped us. He has provided this help in His Son. Jesus Christ is the man who has perfectly walked in the fear of the Lord. At every point, we see Him as the one who is faithful, who has lived the good and perfect life. He is the one who has all knowledge. He is the one who chose the fear of the Lord. He is the one who exerted Himself on earth through fasting and prayer as He grew in wisdom, stature, and favor with God and man. Christ is the one who humbled Himself, not considering equality with God a thing to be grasped but became obedient to death, the death of the cross. Christ is the one who listened to instruction, even as a boy sitting in His Father's house. Christ is the one who has produced abundant life for us to enjoy. He, in the fear of God, had courage to go to the cross, laying His life down for us and for our salvation. He is the one who resisted all greed, saying to Peter, "Get behind me, Satan! For you are not setting your mind on the things of God, but on the things of man" (Mark 8:33). He hated evil, saying to the corrupt Pharisees that they belonged to their father the devil. He walked uprightly as the only one perfectly fulfilling the law of God.

If you would have the fear of God, then you must have the Christ of God.

ENDNOTES

1   Jonathan Edwards, *The Works of Jonathan Edwards*, (New Haven, CT: Yale University Press, 1998), 16:753–54.

2   Jonathan Edwards, *The Works of Jonathan Edwards: The Great Awakening* (New Haven, CT: Yale University Press, 1972), 4:415.

3   Jen Christensen, "Judge gives grandparents custody of Ohio transgender teen," CNN, February 16, 2018, https://www.cnn.com/2018/02/16/health/ohio-transgender-teen-hearing-judge-decision/index.html.

4   Kevin Grasha, "Judge paves way for transgender teen to get hormone therapy at Cincinnati Children's Hospital," Cincinnati.com, February 16, 2018, https://www.cincinnati.com/story/news/2018/02/16/judge-paves-way-transgender-teen-get-hormone-therapy-cincinnati-childrens-hospital/345321002.

5   Charles Bridges, *An Exposition of the Book of Proverbs* (London: R. Carter, 1871), 3.

6   See Thomas Watson's *Doctrine of Repentance* for a full analysis of the subject. This section tracks with some of his thought.

7   Elizabeth Cady Stanton, *The Woman's Bible, Part 2: Comments on the Old and New Testaments from Joshua to Revelation* (New York: European, 1898), 214

8   Gene Veith, "Mallory Millett's Critique of Her Sister's Feminism," Patheos, February 12, 2018, https://www.patheos.com/blogs/geneveith/2018/02/the-other-ms-milletts-withering-critique-of-feminism.

9   Jordan Peterson, "Break the law and see what happens! Jordan Peterson," YouTube, March 21, 2020, https://www.youtube.com/watch?v=AxI5r4_I5uA.

Scripture Index

GENESIS

1:28	1
3:6	46
3:8	112

DEUTERONOMY

32:4	94

JOSHUA

9:4	66
24:15	81

1 CHRONICLES

29:17	31

2 CHRONICLES

20:12	14

JOB

1:21	108

PSALMS

1	77, 90
1:6	25
2	97
5:6	46
7:11	137
7:14	105
14:1	84, 104
16:3	17, 115
16:4	99, 135
16:6	136

16:8	34
19	4
19:1	8, 65
19:7–10	59
24:1	23, 89
63:5–6	75
94:20	16
101:3	34
104:15	75
110:3	87
119:7	31
119:9	65, 113
119:57	135
119:97	12, 59
119:99	12

PROVERBS

1:2	3
1:3	4
1:4	5
1:7	5, 84, 104
1:8	1, 8, 88
1:10	6, 8
1:13	6
1:15	7
1:19	7
1:20–21	8
1:22–23	9
1:24–26	9
1:28	10
1:28–31	133
1:29–30	10
1:32	9
1:33	10
2:1	12
2:1–4	100

HEBREWS

1:3	133
9:27	24
13:4	42
13:17	122

JAMES

1:5	13
1:7–8	13
1:22	1
3:15	105

1 PETER

2:9	1
3:3	124
3:4	60
3:5	60
4:8	112

1 JOHN

1:5–10	117
3:15	6